STAYIN' ALIVE

Stayin' Alive

Armed and Female

In an Unsafe World

By Paxton Quigley

MERRIL PRESS
Bellevue, Washington

Stayin' Alive: Armed and Female in an Unsafe World is published by Merril Press, P.O. Box 1682, Bellevue, WA 98009. Additional copies of this book may be ordered from Merril Press at $15.00 each. Phone: 425-454-7009. Cover Photo by Boxer Productions and Cover Design by Tiffany Lindsay.

FIRST EDITION

LIBRARY OF CONGRESS CATALOGING-IN-PUBLICATION DATA

Quigley, Paxton.
   Stayin' alive: armed and female in an unsafe world / by Paxton
   Quigley.-- 1st ed. p. cm.
   Includes bibliographical references
   ISBN 0-936783-43-5
   1. Self-defense for women--United States. 2. Firearms owners--
   United States. I. Title.

 GV1111.5Q87 2005
 613.6'6082--dc22

                                           2005041509

PRINTED IN THE UNITED STATES OF AMERICA

According to the Department of Justice (1998) 27% of American Women keep a gun in the house and 37.6 million females either own or have rapid access to guns.

IN MEMORY
TO MY DEAR FRIEND, AUTHOR JOHN SACK,
WHO BROUGHT ME GREAT JOY AND HELPED ME
THROUGHOUT MOST OF MY LIFE
1930- 2004

ACKNOWLEDGMENTS

No book is written by one person. Over the years, I have met so many women and men who have given me their knowledge about self-defense and the use of handguns. Although the numbers of individuals who have contributed number in the hundreds, I want to thank certain people who have been paramount in my life. First and foremost, I would like to acknowledge my terrific friends and assistants, Phyliss and Fred Cook, who helped me to train thousands of women in Los Angeles. Others who have worked with me "on the line," who I would like to thank include Nancy Moran Sanchez, Adolph Visconti, Stan Weisleder, Andrew Cooper and all of the other men and women who generously gave their time to help my students on gun ranges in all areas of the country.

I want to especially thank Bob Scott, president, Smith & Wesson, Ken Jorgenson, former public relations director, Smith & Wesson (currently with Ruger) and their associates, who gave me the rare opportunity of being a spokesperson for Smith & Wesson for eleven years and also providing me with Smith & Wesson guns for my seminars.

Also, thanks go to the generosity and friendship of Laura Roberts Niner and Marten Niner, at Pantheon Chemical Company; Jan Lebourel, who gave me the chance to write a "Personal Protection" column for *Handguns* magazine; Don Kates Esq., Mark Benenson, Esq., Helmut Julinot, BJ Julinot, Larry Wilson, Robert Waters, Johann Opitz, John Lott, Alan Gottlieb of the Second Amendment Foundation, the wonderful women at *Women & Guns* magazine, including Peggy Tartaro, Lyn Bates, Karen MacNutt and Gila Hayes. Also, my continued appreciation to Martha Braunig at Executive Security International, Aspen, Colorado and thanks to Jeff Boxer, who photographed the cover of the book.

Additionally, my appreciation to friends, Jeff Mannix, Richard Rosenthal, David Columbia, Max Ramberg, Larry Patterson, Barbara Cohn, Marie Yates, Mel Klein, Allen Baron, Terry and Paul Lichtman, Judy and Arnie Fishman, Mark and Kay Bloom, Allyson Gottfried and her family, Adam, Alan and Marge, and love, to my sons, David and Jonathan and my parents, Hy and Lillian.

Los Angeles, California
2004

$\mathcal{P}$ REFACE

Intruder dies at hands of armed East Sider
By Vincent T. Davis San Antonio Express-
News Web Posted: 11/03/2003 12:00 AM

A 21-year-old man was shot and killed late Saturday on the East Side when he broke through a woman's front window at the Morningview Oaks Apartments.

According to a police report, Ernest Flores III broke through Judy Abram's living room window as she played dominoes with her sisters.

Abram yelled at Flores to leave, but he kept advancing. She ran to her bedroom, grabbed a pistol, and told him she had a gun. When he continued to enter the room, Abram, 55, fired two times while screaming, "Can't you see I have a gun? Get out of here!"

The police report said Flores continued to break through the window as Abram fired the remaining four bullets at him. She dashed to her bedroom to reload, but when she returned, Flores was gone.

Staggering next door, Flores crashed through a neighbor's front window and fell face down on a table where police found him with one gunshot wound to the upper chest.

Police said Abram acted in self-defense and no charges are expected to be filed.

The police report said that prior to the break-in, Flores left a neighbor's house across the street rambling that someone was after him. The neighbor said the last time she saw Flores he was crawling across the street and breaking through Abram's window.

By Sunday afternoon, a maintenance man had replaced the bullet-riddled blinds and two broken windows, but talk of the break-in buzzed on the street. Several children poked their heads into a television news van parked at the location, while residents milled around and compared notes on the incident.
Cont.

Neighbor John W. Prince didn't join those in the street.

The 79-year-old spent Sunday afternoon listening to 1960s soul music with wife Gwenderlyn, 69, in their house on the corner of BookerTee and Morning View.

When asked about the shooting, Prince said when he heard the gunshots he did what he had learned during the Korean War — he automatically hit the floor.

"I can't stand it. It bothers me," Prince said of hearing gunfire.

The 13-year Army veteran and his wife have lived on the corner since the early 1990s, and both said their neighborhood is usually quiet.

"Somebody showed up at the wrong place," he said. "And that's going on around the city."

vtdavis@express-news.net

http://news.mysanantonio.com/
story.cfm?xla=saen&xlb=310&xlc=1078777&xld=310
   11/03/2003

TABLE OF CONTENTS

INTRODUCTION

The illiterate of the 21st century will not be those who cannot read and write, but those who cannot learn, unlearn, and relearn.
— Alvin Toffler

If you worry about your safety, you're not alone. A recent Gallup poll reported that six out of ten women in America are afraid to walk in their own neighborhoods or go out alone at night. For these women, the feeling of an ever-present threat of violence or harm effectively denies them the basic guarantees of life and liberty. And the feeling is more than a perception. It is based on a strong dose of reality; not just what nay-sayers would call a neurotic obsession with danger. The fact is, many women in America really are at constant risk. They are victims of society's disquieting inability to protect women from violence and harm inside or outside their own homes.

The female fear factor is doubly destructive because it makes women not only victims of their attackers, but of their own fear-oriented thinking as well.

Ironically, most women are just too afraid to take responsibility and prepare themselves against a possible life-threatening situation. They shrink from learning how to protect themselves even when they are given the chance. Over the years, I have spoken about self-defense gun training with no end of women who rejected it, who came up with a variety of lame excuses as to why they didn't want to learn. Excuses often echo messages in the media spawned by influential organizations, such as the American Public Health Association, the American Academy of Pediatrics, the Harvard School of Public Health, the Centers for Disease Control and Protection, and the American Medical Association. Well-meaning as these groups may be, they issue skewed, half-digested statistics that twist the facts and increase the chances of further female victimization. Sadly, the messages from these prominent groups are all-too-often accepted by the media and the unsuspecting as gospel.

I've seen the problem from a different perspective. I've been in the unique position of teaching nearly 7,000 women in over ten years in more than 20 states how to shoot a handgun for self-defense. As a result, I have had a chance to witness powerful attitude changes from most of these newly-trained women.

Whether they're 20 or 50 years old, they usually come to my seminars with enormous psychological trepidation, a sense that guns are somehow evil, a tool of the devil. I always applaud them for breaking through a gigantic mental barrier to learn how to use a piece of equipment—that's all it is—that has long been an instrument of power excluded to women, until now.

When a woman first grips a loaded gun, her palms sweat and her heart races. When she fires that first shot into a paper silhouette target at a distance of seven feet, her startle reflex is activated by the gun's blast and its "kick," but soon she realizes after firing round after round that <u>she controls</u> the tool—the handgun doesn't control her. She's in charge and sometimes, it's for the first time in her life that she's in charge! Some women are so excited they hoot and yell, "You go, girl. Don't mess with us!"

That's what the 50 women at Mount Holyoke College, an Ivy League women's institution, pronounced implicitly when they started the first college chapter of the Second Amendment Sisters, a national pro-gun women's organization, in March 2002. The group motivated impassioned exchanges in the student newspaper and on e-mail chat groups.

"You can't achieve power by using guns," exclaimed Jean Grossholtz, an emeritus professor at the college and chair of the women's studies program. "When women can take their rightful place in the world as who they are, not as little make-believe men, that's women's liberation."

Their presence caused the college president, Beverly Daniel Tatum, to issue a special statement reassuring alumnae that members of the woman's group don't carry guns on campus. That, of course, would violate state law.

They attracted considerable national media attention. *The New York Times'* columnist, Nicholas Kirstoff grumbled that college girls were now shooting guns and blamed it on the 9/11/01 attacks, rather than taking into account that women have every right to protect themselves and know how to shoot a gun. Although he himself had been brought up with guns in Oregon and was "comfortable" with them, his comfort level didn't apparently extend to women and he insinuated that more people would be killed.

Mr. Kristoff would today acknowledge that he overreacted. He was however, right that September 11 provoked many people, and particularly women, to reconsider their position on the gun issue. According to the National Shooting Sports Foundation, there's been a 25% surge in gun sales since that fatal day and women have accounted for roughly 60% of the increase!

Lt. Police Officer Margot Hill, the commander of Boston's domestic-violence unit, said she wasn't surprised to hear more women seemed to be interested in having a gun for protection after September 11. "It was a wake-up call to everyone. People felt that the government couldn't protect them."

Most of these new women gun-owners aren't politically motivated, but propelled by the most basic of female instincts—the urge to protect their own, their families and themselves against harm from those who threaten them. After years of just being scared, awakening to the reality of the dangers faced today as Americans, and as women, women have produced a compelling desire to take action and try to do something about it. Women living alone, working late, or raising children are beginning to look at guns in an entirely different light. They're getting over the blind fear and terror of guns and the media's wholesale demonization of gun-owners, and beginning to realize that the subject is not so black and white, good or bad as it's painted by antigun activists. Despite the nay-sayers skepticism and scorn, women are also seeing that there may be more than a little truth to the maxim that it's not the gun itself, but the person holding it who matters—who controls how the gun is used or misused.

With the specter of homicide bombers in our midst no longer just a remote fantasy, women may actually be able to take a role in American homeland defense. Crazy, you say? Hardly. In Israel, where the government has issued more than 60,000 gun permits so ordinary citizens can help stop attackers who try to set off bombs, an Israeli housewife in 2002 saved countless lives when she shot dead a terrorist about to set off an explosive device in an Efrat supermarket. The terrorist died. How many innocent men, women and children would have died if this woman had not been trained in how to use a gun?

This is a book about women finally coming to the awareness that they must free themselves from years of foolish, naïve, fatalistic illusions of incompetence and invulnerability and use the tools that have been available to men. Millions of maverick women have learned how to free themselves, and millions more need to do it. It's high time women took aim at their outdated behavior and realized they can seize the initiative and play a strong role in protecting themselves and their loved ones in an increasingly dangerous world.

Nonetheless, this is not an anti-male book. It would be wrong of me to say that all women are innocent or are victims. Crimes against people, as well as domestic violence is not just a male's "privilege." Unfortunately, women do perpetrate crime out on the streets and particularly, in their homes. Recent studies sponsored by the National Institutes of Health (2003) have found that many women can be the aggressors and "hit first" against their partner or spouse.

The research said they did not blame women. "We are not saying anybody is at fault," said Miriam Ehrensaft of

Columbia University. "But new data is emerging that says women are also involved in aggression. If we do not tell women that, we put them at risk."

The studies' researchers called for a re-evaluation of treatment programs nationwide. One of the researchers, Deobrah Capaldi of the Oregon Social Learning Center said, "Prevention and treatment should focus on managing conflict and aggression for both young men and women. Each needs to understand the role both play while still putting a 'special responsibility' on the man, who can inflict greater injury."

Nevertheless, women continue to be the primary victims in these domestic violence cases. I hope that as our society becomes more open to the causes of domestic violence and deals with the issue, women will not be prone to victim-hood.

Fortunately, new state laws are being passed to help battered women and more governors are granting clemency to imprisoned women, who have killed their husbands or boyfriends. California has enacted a unique law (SB 1385) in 2004 that states that if battered women can prove their abusers coerced them into committing violent crimes (other than killing their abusers), they will have a chance to win release under this legislation. (The new law also applies to men.) It also allows those who killed their spouses between 1992, when California passed its initial battered defense law, and August 29, 1996, when the state Supreme Court ratified it, to seek new trials.

All women should encourage their state officials to grant more of these clemency decisions and to enact laws similar to California's new legislation. In the interim, women need to take care of themselves and learn to be responsible for their safety and the safety of their loved ones.

CHAPTER ONE
WHY GUNS FOR WOMEN?

"Nothing more simple, I assure you...But I'll tell you what. You must have your mind, your nerve, and everything in harmony. Don't look at your gun, simply follow the object with the end of it, as if the tip of the barrel was the point of your finger."
- Annie Oakley

A recent rash of neighborhood burglaries and assaults had Barbara and her friends unnerved and quietly admitting to themselves that they were scared. The consensus was that they hated feeling so vulnerable, and a fed-up few had actually resolved to take the bull by the horns and do something "real" about it.

A single parent, too, Barbara investigated the possibility of getting a home alarm system, but decided against it when she was told that "alarms are just alarms," and should be viewed as warning devices. Barbara thought about joining her neighbors in purchasing a handgun for self-protection, but with three kids in the house, she held back. Except what if whomever had broken into her garage three times over the past few months decided to go further? Sure, they'd only swiped bicycles and toys at first, but just a few weeks ago she'd come home to find they'd taken the time to clean out the whole freezer.

"My intuition told me whoever was doing this was very comfortable, very confident about how and when we come and go, " Barbara explained, "and that freaked me out."

She finally overcame her doubts and ventured forth to a Chicago area gun store where she bought a shiny new snub-nosed Rossi .38 special caliber, along with a red plastic trigger lock that the salesman showed her how to brace behind and in front of the trigger so the gun wouldn't fire accidentally if by some chance, the kids managed to get a hold of it.

On the way home, Barbara smiled to herself. She'd done the right thing. Now at least, she'd be prepared for that horrible, unthinkable *I-hope-and-pray-it-never-happens-but-just-in-case* moment. For security and easy access, she decided she'd keep her new purchase safely tucked under her mattress.

Months later, Barbara lay in bed nursing a cold, 2-year-old Kendall at her side. Her teenage daughter had made it off to school, but son, Eric had also felt under the weather and was still home. Around 8 am., Barbara heard the doorbell ring.

"Mama!" Eric yelled. "There's a man at the door. He's saying something about some keys."

Barbara got up from the bed, adjusted her ankle-length nightshirt and went downstairs. She didn't open the door, but peered through the top window glass and saw a big man in jeans and a flannel shirt.

"Your daughter has my car keys from my son," the man said, telling of a friendship between her daughter and a boy Barbara had never heard of.

"I dunno," Barbara said. "My daughter is only 15 and she's at school right now. I'll talk to her when she gets home."

The man nodded, and Barbara watched him turn and leave the front yard. A few hours later, the doorbell rang again.

"Mama," Eric called. "That man is here again." Barbara got out of bed. This time, little Kendall toddled after her.

"We found the keys," the man said. "But I think there's something you need to see," as he pulled out a folded paper from his pocket. "This letter that your daughter wrote to my son," he said, holding the folded paper up against the glass.

Curious, Barbara unlocked the door and opened it just far enough to push the latch on the screen door and take the offered letter. She pulled the screen door closed but left the wooden inner door open - just a crack.

"Uh, this isn't my daughter's..." was all Barbara could say before the man was coming down on her with a 6-inch rusty blade, jabbing it into her flesh. He held the knife, now bloody, over her. "I'm going to kill you," he breathed, thrusting it again and again as she fell to the floor.

Eleven-year-old Eric jumped on the man's back, locking his thin arms around the man's neck. The assailant bit his hand as they wrestled. The boy howled, but somehow managed to hang on while little Kendall just screamed.

Suddenly, Barbara remembered the gun. Slipping and stumbling in her own blood, she ran off toward the bedroom, slammed the door and locked it behind her. She got to the bed, reached under and grabbed the gun in her now bloody hands. Desperately, she tried pulling the lock off and realized she needed the key which she'd stashed under an exercise machine next to the bed. After several attempts, the key rotated in the cylinder, popping the plastic lock free.

"I'm going to stop this mother fucker right now!" she said to herself running downstairs.

"Get away from my children!" she screamed, mopping the blood from her face with her sleeve.

Spying the object in her hand, the attacker turned, ran through the dining room to the window and drew back his elbow to smash it through just as Barbara pulled the trigger.

Bam! Bam! Bam! The man's body spun as she kept firing until she'd emptied the chamber. He slowly slid to the floor in a heap as she ran to the phone and called 911 bringing an ambulance and the police in a matter of minutes.

The man, Johnny Jones was 37 when he'd attacked Barbara and her sons. Twenty years earlier, he'd been locked up for raping two women but had somehow been released after only four years served for "good behavior." Out only a few months, he was again arrested, convicted of aggravated battery and rape, and sentenced to 26 years in prison. There, he confessed to a couple of murders for which he was sentenced to another 27 years by a judge who unaccountably ordered that the murder sentence be served concurrently with the rape term. Fourteen years later, Johnny Jones was paroled, and not long thereafter showed up at Barbara's door ready to kill again.

When the judge finally sentenced Jones to spend the rest of his natural life in prison, declaring him "a menace, a career criminal, an urban predator..." Barbara could only think, "better late than never." Except the gun she'd used to save herself and her family was now gone, tucked away on a shelf somewhere in a plastic bag labeled "evidence."

Undeterred by her initial experience, Barbara went right out and purchased a new gun because "the world we live in is just too darn dangerous not to be as prepared as we can."

While we like to think of America as a civilized country and ourselves as a civilized people, the fact is crime and violence remain rampant producing tens of millions of innocent victims each and every year. No matter how many laws are passed, there will always be those for whom they have no meaning and serve as no deterrent. Those who believe otherwise have their heads dangerously in the clouds.

Jaquie Creazzo, 31, was a recently divorced mother of three, living in a small town outside Boulder, Colorado when she left home at 5:30 one cold, icy February morning to pick up her father. Nearing an off-ramp on the Boulder Turnpike, she saw two cars stopped up ahead, emergency flashers blinking and two figures standing there.

"The woman suddenly bolted from the man and started running downhill towards me," recalled Jaquie. "She wasn't screaming, but she had such a look of dread on her face I instantly knew she needed help."

Jaquie slowed and the woman jumped in the passenger seat shouting hysterically that a man with a gun was trying to kill her.

The woman, Rhonda Maloney, a 25-year-old cocktail waitress at a Denver casino had worked until 2 AM, gotten into her car and started home to her husband when she was bumped by another car and forced off the road. At first the other driver, Robert Harlan, had offered to help, but then raped her and held her captive for hours.

Seeing Harlan now jump in his car and head off after them, Jaquie decided to make for the police station just two exits away. The cars raced along for a while until Harlan pulled even on the driver's side, pointed a gun and started shooting. Jaquie floored it but Harlan came up on her again and kept firing repeatedly at the women.

Unaware at the time that bullets had slammed into her mouth, knee and spine, adrenaline pumping, Jaquie reached the police station and careened up on the lawn about a half-block from the front door. Then she passed out. She didn't see Harlan pull Rhonda out of the car and throw her to the ground but came to long enough to see him return again to grab Rhonda's purse and vest.

"I got a real good look at him and he looked at me. This was the face that I thought was going to kill me so it was burned into my head,"

For the next 45 minutes, Jaquie faded in and out of consciousness until a police officer reporting for duty finally noticed her car and she was able to tell what had happened.

Two days later, the police found and arrested Robert Harlan. A week later, Rhonda's body was discovered under a bridge, the victim of repeated blows to the head and several gunshot wounds.

Jaquie was not expected to survive, but surprised everyone. A bullet had entered her mouth and knocked out her teeth, but far worse was the one lodged in her 5th lumbar vertebra that paralyzed her from mid-chest down and would force her to spend the rest of her life in a wheelchair.

After many agonizing months in a rehab hospital and multiple surgeries, Jaquie was finally able to return home to her three young daughters.

Robert Harlan was a 29-year-old telephone operator at US West where for the prior seven years, dozens of female employees had claimed they were stalked, intimidated, sexually abused and harassed by him. Although he had earlier been convicted of three sex-related offenses, a prior arrest for rape led to a mistrial when the victim refused to testify. After the Rhonda Maloney incident, Harlan became the #1 suspect in the beating death of a co-worker at US West.

As the prime witness against Harlan at his trial for the murder of Rhonda Maloney, Jaquie feared his friends might try to stop her from testifying or seek retribution later on. Aware the police could only do so much and would not be able to assure her safety, Jaquie considered all of her options and finally decided she had no real choice but to buy a handgun and learn how to use it.

Today, in a fanny pack strapped to Jaquie's wheelchair is a loaded gun. At night, the chair, fanny pack and its contents sit at the ready, next to her bed. While she hopes never to have to use it, knowing she's not entirely vulnerable and can defend herself if necessary is a bittersweet comfort for Jaquie.

Generally speaking, aside from sports shooting, women own and use a gun almost exclusively for self-defense. Of the 26,000 homicides in U.S. in 2000, more than 90% were committed by males. Each year, some 4,000 American women are murdered, mostly by men.

While overall violent crimes have decreased slightly over the last few years, lo and behold, the number of reported rapes has actually increased! The FBI said in its annual Uniform Crime Report that crime nationwide fell 0.2% in 2002, but rape went up 4.0% with the Northeast leading the nation by a 6.2% increase.

In 2000, the Justice Department's National Crime Victimization Survey claims there were only 261,000 *reported* victims of sexual assault, attempted or completed rape. Except the FBI says only 35% of rapes are ever reported and estimates something like 1.2 million rapes were committed in the U.S. in 2000, which averages out to more than 3,300 every day of the year.

Experts do agree that approximately one out of every six American women have been or will be the victim of an attempted or completed rape during their lifetimes.

What's extra horrifying is that if 2/3's of all rapes and sexual assaults are **not** reported, all those bad guys are still out there, emboldened by their successes and ready for more.

Why do so many rapes go unreported? According to the 2000 National Crime Victimization Survey, most victims just fear retribution from the assailant or his family and friends! And even when they do initially report an assault to the police, they often don't follow through because they're too frightened to testify and their cases are dropped.

One such casualty is Michelle Robinson who ended up in an Indianapolis jail cell while her rapist was released without even having to post bail. Yes, you read that correctly.

Robertson, 34, a mother of a grade-school child was attacked by a knife-wielding two-time sex-crime felon, who came through her bedroom window at night. For months afterwards, she had nightmares reliving the attack.

Too scared to testify in open court, she had missed three prior appointments to give her statement in the presence of the defense attorney, so Judge Patricia Gifford issued a warrant for her arrest for failing to appear as a material witness.

"Nobody wants to make a victim into a victim twice," the judge said, "but unfortunately, within our system of justice, to make it all work, you need to come to court to testify. By not appearing, the case becomes impossible. And as a result of her not appearing, the defendant had to be released, which I don't think anyone thought should happen."

Beth Gelhausen, director of the Prevail Victim Assistance Program was shocked and said trials are "incredibly traumatic" for sex-assault victims. "I can picture this woman being dressed, ready to go and not being able to walk out of her bathroom. I've seen victims become physically ill and not be able to do this."

"I've never been in jail before" said Michelle. "I was in a big cell with about 20 other women. It's a black hole – hard metal beds, no pillows or mats. They don't care if you sleep on the floor."

The moment of truth came when she finally got out of jail the next day, was brought into court and had to walk right past her attacker. "I looked over at him," Michelle confided. "And then I knew I could do it." Soon after, her rapist was found guilty and is currently in prison.

Many other women are not victims of chance circumstances but of ongoing violent relationships, from which escape is difficult or seemingly impossible.

One such example occurred in Chicago on Wednesday, May 3, 2002, just before midnight, when Ronyale White's estranged husband threatened to kill her. She called 911 at 11:40 p.m. screaming that he was outside the house and that she had a restraining order that was supposed to be given "Priority 1A" status by the police department.

After the operator told her the police were on their way, Ronyale locked her bedroom door and activated a tape recorder. Five minutes later, she called again saying her husband had a gun and was warning her she was going to die.

In her third and last call at 11:50 p.m., she pleaded for the police to arrive as a helpless operator heard a man's voice threatening death, followed by a loud noise, like a door being kicked in. Seconds later, two shots were heard and the phone went dead. Police arrived at Ronyale's house at 11:57 p.m. - almost 17 minutes after the initial call - and found Ronyale dead on the floor.

Would Ronyale be alive today if she had a gun and

knew how to use it? Probably. She had time to lock her bedroom door and turn on a tape recorder, so she would have had the opportunity to load her gun and be ready when her enraged husband started threatening her before he kicked the door in.

Sharlotte Pearson, a domestic violence victim, was prepared. After taking the police department's advice, Sharlotte moved to Forest Park, Florida from Pensacola to escape her former husband, Marvin Pearson, who had beaten her repeatedly both before and after their marriage. But, he soon found her. On a cool late fall evening, she returned from work and her niece told her that Marvin and her niece's boyfriend, Wallace, had gone to the store for food. "I felt I was in great trouble," explained Sharlotte, so she decided to get her gun from the attic, loaded it, and put it in her bedroom drawer.

When the two men returned, things appeared peaceful until Marvin took her into the bedroom where they began arguing and then fighting. He hit her and bit her on the lip after telling her not to scream. He continued to beat her even after waking up their youngest son who was on the bed asleep in the same room.

Sharlotte shouted to Wallace to call the police. When Marvin ran to stop Wallace from making the call, she got her gun. The two men briefly fought and Marvin ran into the bedroom. Determined to stop him, Sharlotte shot and killed him.

She was arrested and charged with murder. At her trial on May 23, 2002, her lawyer said, "this trial is about a bully, a bully who had beat on her and beat on her and beat on her some more. Sharlotte Pearson said don't tread on me, leave me alone."

After hearing a day and a half of evidence, the jury took just 30 minutes to find Sharlotte not guilty. "Now I can raise my boys," Sharlotte happily declared just before calling her mother to tell her the news.

"What I had to do had nothing to do with shooting or murder; what I did had to be done for my safety and the safety of my kids," said Sharlotte, smiling for the first time after her grueling time in court. She has returned her gun to the attic, but as she said, "it's there for me if God forbid, I need it."

A gun can also be a great deterrent and there are many stories of mavericks—women, who have stopped attacks without having to shoot their weapons. One man learned the hard way to never to cross his mother-in-law, especially if she has a permit to carry a gun.

One Saturday afternoon on January 7, 2003, in Atlanta, Georgia, Jim Halston, 41, dragged his estranged wife, Denny, from her mother's car. While she kicked and screamed, he carried her into his house where he punched her on the right side of her head. Denny's mother pulled out her handgun from her purse and ran into the unlocked house where she ordered Halston to sit on the floor until the police arrived.

Halston was arraigned on charges of simple assault, harassment and a charge of indirect criminal contempt, which stemmed from a "protection from abuse order" signed 10 days prior to the altercation, which ordered Hill not to have any contact with his wife.

After Denny received medical care, she said that she knew that her mother was carrying a gun, but she never thought that her mother would be her "savior." "I've been beat up so much by him," she explained, "that I thought this may be the time when he would kill me, but my mom knew what to do."

According to the U.S. Department of Justice (1998) 27% of American women keep a gun in the house and 37.6 million females either own or have rapid access to guns. That's a lot of women, but the majority of women don't have guns.

Over the years, women have asked me, "What can I do if I don't want a gun?" I explain that there are other options, but in the end the smartest way to protect oneself is with a gun. It is by far the most powerful weapon a woman can have for self protection. Of course, I understand that even if you have a gun, you may not be able to use it or you may hot have it in your possession, so it is crucial to have other alternatives.

The following chapter offers options that can be effective for preventing an assault.

CHAPTER TWO
OTHER SELF DEFENSE OPTIONS

"Live as brave men (women);
and if fortune is adverse,
front its blows with brave hearts."
- Cicero

A gun is not an all-purpose self defense device. A gun should only be used for particular, life-threatening situations, which includes the possibility of rape.

Furthermore, even if you have your gun on you or near you, you may not be able to use it for a variety of reasons, including the risk of wounding or even killing others.

That's why I recommend that all women take self defense classes that teach the basics of learning how to fight using their bodies. Years ago, it was difficult to find these types of classes, but now practically every city offers a myriad of programs. I always advise that the earlier in life you've taken a course, the better chance you have of not being a criminal target. If nothing else, you learn to become an aware individual, which is half the battle of not being victimized. If you're a mother with children as young as five years old, I suggest that you find a class for both your sons and daughters. They'll have a good time and they'll learn the meaning and feeling of personal empowerment.

PEPPER SPRAY

A student of mine, Elana Solera, was accosted one early morning in a hospital parking structure. "I had to go to the Long Beach Hospital at about 1 a.m. because my sister was having a baby. I wasn't particularly nervous, but I parked as near as possible to the entrance to the door, and still had to walk about 100 feet," she explained. "Without even thinking, I always carry my pepper spray on my key chain for that just-in-case situation. That night was one of those situations. I must have taken about ten steps when this guy came out in front of a car. He yelled at me and started toward me."

Elana doesn't remember how long it took him to get to her, but she raised the small canister and squeezed the button squirting a stream that hit the guy's eyes. He started moaning and wiping his hands on his face, and then he collapsed. Elana ran into the hospital screaming for help and a security officer ran to her. "We went out to the parking structure and the guy was still down on the ground! I always knew it was powerful stuff, and I saw it in action," said Elana, who bought a fresh canister the next day, hoping never to use it again.

Pepper spray (or pepper foam) is considered to be a nonlethal weapon and is designed to incapacitate an attacker <u>instantly</u> without after-affects. The product goes under various brand names and different formulas. Some are made by reliable companies, others aren't. Pepper spray contains an oleoresin capsicum solution, an all-natural substance, better known as cayenne pepper, which is derived from various hot red pepper plants. When sprayed properly—whether in stream, cone-of-mist, or burst units—it has a devastating short-term effect on humans, regardless of their intoxicated or emotional condition. The pepper causes the membranes to swell, producing instant eye closure, uncontrollable coughing, gagging and the sensation of intense burning to the skin. Also, it contracts the diaphragm causing the attacker to double over, often halting him in mid-stride.

I've spoken to police officers, who've been pepper-sprayed as part of their training, and they all report that the pain was so intense that they never wanted to be sprayed again! Fred Cook, a Los Angeles area police officer says, "getting hit with pepper, is like putting your hand on a hot stove and not being able to take it off. The pain keeps intensifying."

It's important to spray to the attacker's face. The ideal range of spraying is within four to six feet of an attacker.

Spraying the canister at distances of <u>less</u> than two feet can cause incomplete evaporation of the spray and can retard the full effect of the active agent for as long as 30 seconds—much too long of a time when being assaulted.

Unfortunately, it has its limitations. If it's raining, snowing or very windy, the spray may be ineffective and not hit the target or if the wind is blowing in your direction, you, rather than the attacker, may be affected by the spray. And indoors, the spray may disable everyone!

A number of years ago, I was giving a seminar for 300 employees in the ballroom of a large hotel in Waikiki, Hawaii, when one of the attendees pulled out a small pepper spray canister to show the woman sitting next to her and she accidentally pushed the canister's button squirting the pepper spray into the air. Within a minute, people started choking and coughing, including me while I stood on the stage at least sixty feet away from the spray's burst! Everyone had to evacuate the room and returned about 15 minutes later after the air conditioning was put on full blast.

If a training class is available in your community in the usage of pepper spray, do take it. Even though you'll use spray canisters filled with an inert liquid, you'll develop a sense of how accurately you can spray an attacker, and at what distance. One squirt of spray may not knock down your assailant. Know that you may need to continue spraying before the attacker is down.

If there isn't a class, check out the various pepper spray companies online and purchase an inert canister. It allows you to rehearse scenarios with a friend, who can attack you from different positions, including from behind. Practice pulling the canister out of your pocket, purse or key-chain. Get to know the feel of the canister so you know which way the spray nozzle is pointed. It's a good way to ascertain how quickly you react in a crisis situation. Practice spraying numerous times.

I do recommend that you make it a habit while walking to carry your small canister in your strong hand in a ready position. As soon as you perceive a threat, place your thumb on the spray's actuator, so you'll be ready to spray. If you're fighting with the attacker, it may be extremely difficult to get your canister out of your purse or pocket.

What do you do after you've sprayed the attacker? Does he fall into a heap moaning and crying while you watch? Not necessarily so. He could react in a deranged and violent way. Self-defense expert Massad Ayoob, who trains police officers in the use of sprays, recommends that you simulate the worst-case scenario during your training and practice moving backward or sideway and spraying again to the attacker's face. After that, Ayoob advises that you divert your movement so that if the attacker carries on his assault he most probably will strike toward the position where last he saw you.

You can carry pepper spray canisters across most state-lines. Unfortunately, you can't take these products on planes, even in checked luggage. Changing air pressures at high altitudes can cause the canisters to leak and could destroy your clothes and cosmetics. Buy a canister at your destination point and when you leave, give it to someone. If you discard it, don't be careless, since you don't want a child to find it and use it. And that reminds me, if you do have young children, you must be careful to keep it away from them. If your children are curious or unruly, I suggest you think twice about acquiring a spray product.

If you or one of your children is accidentally sprayed, the symptoms can be relieved by flushing the eyes with cool water, going outside for fresh air, and washing the entire body and hair with soap and cold water. Left untreated, the symptoms should stop in 15 to 45 minutes. If not, call a doctor. If the spray has been discharged indoors normal ventilation will remove the spray in 45 minutes. Clothing that's been sprayed should be washed or cleaned.

Canisters are available in different sizes and can be purchased through catalogues, hardware stores, drug stores or at gun stores. There are more than 100 sprays on the market, so be careful what you buy. There should be a minimum of 10 seconds' total continuous discharge of spray and a ten percent content of oleoresin capsicum with a 2 million or more SHU rating. This information should be stated on the manufacturer's instructions.

Most states allow pepper spray. However, in Michigan, the law states that pepper spray can be no stronger than 2% OC, which makes it ineffective. In Wisconsin, a UV dye is not allowed and citizens can buy only one state-approved brand, PepperGuard Pepper Spray. In New York, pepper spray can only be purchased from a state licensed firearms dealer or pharmacist and in Massachusetts, a purchaser can only buy from a licensed firearms dealer and must acquire a Firearms Identification card (FID).

STUN GUNS

I've talked to a number of women who carry stun guns and I've warned them that a stun gun doesn't offer "distance defense," like pepper spray does, since you can only use it once the attacker is next to you.

It's not easy to use. A stun gun, which sends out a charge of electricity, only works if the victim manages to firmly hold it while pushing the button and digging the small electrodes into the attacker's body for up to four seconds. Frankly, I don't of know any assailant who will allow his victim to do that, although I have heard of stories where the attackers were immune to the bolts of electricity because they were previously electrocuted. Most probably, he will grab the stun.

What does a stun gun do? It is designed to scramble the nervous system. The resulting energy loss makes it difficult for the attacker to move. It must make contact with the skin or body. Touching an attacker with the two metal prongs on the stun gun quickly causes temporary loss of balance and mental confusion. The longer the unit maintains contact with the attacker's body, the more effective the device is in repelling the attacker. For 1-2 seconds will cause muscle spasms and a dazed mental state. For 3-5 seconds will cause loss of balance and muscle control, total mental confusion and disorientation leaving him dazed for up to fifteen minutes giving the victim a chance to run away. Rarely does it cause cardiac arrest. You cannot suffer a charge-back to your own body—that means you can feel safe when using the device even if the assailant is touching you.

Even if a child were to use the device and apply it to themselves, their muscles would go limp in 1/1000th of a second, causing them to immediately drop it. Stun guns are not toys, and like guns, should be stored away from children.

Rather than using it as a weapon, I think it's more useful as a deterrent. Let's say you're in an underground parking lot and you feel threatened by someone coming toward you, you could warn him to stay away while you hold up the stun gun at eye level, push the button which fires the crackling, bright blue bolts of electricity across the electrodes. You and your stun gun could stop the person from coming any closer to you and giving you a chance to get away.

Available in assorted sizes and different amounts of voltage from 25,000 to l00,000 volts, stun guns can be purchased in gun stores. They are not legal in all states, so check with your local police department before purchasing a stun gun.

MINI-BATONS

I always carry a black mini-baton (also known as the Kubotan) in my purse and use it for my keys. It's a solid plastic ribbed dowel three and a half inches long and three-eighths in diameter with a key-chain on one end (but, you shouldn't keep your small pepper spray canister on it). Designed by a leading master martial arts instructor, Shihan Tahuyuki Kubota, the mini-baton is used by police, prison guards, other law enforcement personnel and savvy women.

To use it defensively, you need to be trained. I was fortunate to meet and be taught by Kubota in his Glendale, California, studio where he taught me various wrist-take downs and neck-lock take-downs, as well as how to use the baton as a handle to slash across an attacker's face and eyes. But, I must admit that I didn't feel secure executing the techniques after the four-hour personal training. It would have taken me many weeks if not months of practice with another person to master the defensive moves.

I recommend that women use the mini-baton as a deterrent rather than as a fighting device. Whenever I don't feel particularly safe whether walking on the streets or in parking lots, malls, and other public places, including elevators, I carry it in my strong hand with the six keys dangling down. The mini-baton certainly makes a statement. I've noticed many people, especially men, cautiously eyeing it when I carry it.

A few years ago, I entered an elevator in New York's Flatiron office building holding my mini-baton in my left hand and a man followed me. As we ascended, he looked at the baton and asked me, "Are you a police officer?" I said no and focused my attention on the elevator panel. There was a long pause. Then, he said, "ma'am, don't worry. I'm in law enforcement. I know what it is," as he gestured toward the baton. "You're smart to carry one in New York."

Many of my students have reported similar stories. Besides functioning as a deterrent, the mini-baton can be a symbol to its owner. One of my students told me that when she holds the mini-baton it prompts her to be aware of her surroundings.

Since the mini-baton plus the keys is rather weighty, I don't use it in the car ignition, nor do I leave it with a car attendant. I always use another set of car keys for my car. And by the way, because the mini-baton is large, I never have a problem finding my keys in my purse!

Plastic mini-batons are legal to carry in the U.S. and I've never had a problem taking mine through airport security; however, I've heard that metal mini-batons have been confiscated.

You can purchase mini-batons for under $10 at gun stores and through mail order. They come in most colors, but black is most intimidating.

DOGS

If you don't already have a dog, consider owning one. Studies indicate that houses with dogs are less likely to be burglarized than homes without them.

Also, the chances of being car-jacked are lessened if you take your dog in your car. Most criminals will pass up an auto with a snarling German Shepherd in the back-seat. Additionally, the likelihood of you being attacked is diminished when you're walking with a large dog. I recommend that real estate agents, traveling saleswomen, and women who work in unsafe areas take their big dogs with them.

There are two categories of dogs I'm talking about. A **watchdog** requires the least training. It can be big or small. This dog barks insistently when an entry is attempted and lets the intruder know that he's been detected, and if you're home it usually goes to the entry point to alert you where the break-in is occurring. By giving warning of an intruder's presence, a watchdog allows you the time to take protective or defensive measures.

One of the easiest ways to train a watchdog, is to chain it to a tree when it's about six months of age. If possible, ask a stranger to invade the dog's territory and then run away. Then, praise the dog excessively. Do this drill a few times a day for a week and soon it will know to bark when a stranger comes near your house, yard or car.

For the great majority of people, a protection-trained dog is quite adequate. A **protection dog** has advanced training. On your command, it barks and lunges at an aggressor. Depending on the training it may or may not actually bite. Also, upon your command, it immediately sits and is silent.

According to Kent, Washington dog trainer and self defense instructor Timothy Maynard, a protection trained dog is "not a "toy" to be shown and displayed as a source of authority. Keep it to yourself and use it only for emergencies. People tend to develop attitudes and as soon as a local jogger or child gets bitten by an unidentified pooch, it will suddenly start to look 'just like your dog'!"

"A protection dog is not an asset without the knowledge required to maintain the training," says Maynard. "A protection dog must be maintained or the asset of protection becomes a liability for your home owner's insurance."

"A protection trained dog is not a cure all for personal security. This does not give you cause to go to "crack infested" areas and peddle Tupperware, or increase your mountain bike workout. The fact that you have a protection trained dog is no different than a handgun. I tell all my students that this (gun or dog) is an excuse to STAY out of trouble. Common sense rules here friends, without that all the guns, knives, ninjas and protection dogs in the world can't help you!"

Don't expect a small dog to be an effective protection dog. They're best for warning of danger. You want a dog that weighs at least 50 pounds. I recommend buying from a reputable breeder a Doberman, a Rottweiller, a German Shepherd, Great Dane, an Akita or a Rhodesian Ridgeback for protection training. Expect to spend $500 to $5,000. If you can't afford these prices, large mixed breeds are just as good and many are more emotionally stable than the larger registered dogs.

One of the best dog training available is Schutzhund, which was begun in Germany and has chapters worldwide. If your dog is exceptionally good in terms of temperament, you and your dog can get involved in various levels of Schutzhund competition, which can be especially rewarding and fun. (Click-on: www.germanshepherddog.com or for all breeds, www.dvgamerica.com)

The trained and maintained protection dog is an asset when compared to the untrained dog. Most dogs have a natural instinct to protect, but in today's environment teaching the dog to trust when and when not to protect is imperative. Protection dogs provide a physical first line of defense, allowing you time to get away, phone 911, or even to round up family members to get them into a safe room until the police arrive, or to respond with lethal force if needed.

According to Maynard, "the security dog in the home requires some forethought. All entry doors and gates must be posted "Beware of Dog" and a warning given if you have a chance. 'If you don't get away/out of my house/ away from my car my dog WILL protect me'. A warning effort will go over well in court. The signs show a willingness to warn bad guys. The vicious dog signs WILL be used against you, as the defendant's lawyer will say you knew you had a mean dog and refer to a picture of the sign."

For other dog training schools, consult your phone directory.

KNIVES AND DAGGERS

Forget about using knives and daggers unless you've taken a special course. If you're not well-trained, the attacker can take a knife away from you and use it against you. Federal, state, and local laws prohibit carrying really effective weapons, so those interested in carrying knives for self-defense must settle for something less.

IMPROVISED WEAPONS

Almost everything in your environment is a possible weapon. Don't be afraid to grab and smash with glasses, bottles, hammers, clipboards, staplers, pots, lamps, chairs, tables, pool cues, flashlights, golf clubs and baseball bats.

You can toss at your attacker your coat, paper clips,

coins, ash tray, sand, dirt, and plates of food, drinks, salt or pepper. A pen, pencil, fork, spoon, ruler, knitting needle, umbrella tip and screwdriver can be pushed into soft areas of an attacker's body. Go for the face with the edge of a credit card, key, knife, comb, box cutter, CD, or fingernail clipper. To gain distance, consider taking off your belt and swinging at your attacker in a figure eight pattern.

YOUR CHECKS

The next time you order checks have only your initials (instead of first name) and last name put on them

If someone takes your check book they will not know if you sign your checks with just your initials or your first name, but your bank will know how you sign your checks.

When you are writing checks to pay on your credit card accounts, DO NOT put the complete account number on the "For" line. Instead, just put the last four numbers. The credit card company knows the rest of the number and anyone who might be handling your check as it passes through all the check processing channels won't have access to it.

Put your work phone number on your checks instead of your home phone. If you have a PO Box use that instead of your home address. If you do not have a PO Box use your work address.

Never print your Social Security number on your checks

Place the contents of your wallet on a photocopy machine, do both sides of each license, credit card, etc. You will know what you had in your wallet and all of the account numbers and phone numbers to call and cancel.

Keep the photocopy in a safe place. Carry a photocopy of your passport when you travel in either the US or abroad.

WALLET STOLEN? HERE'S WHAT TO DO IF YOU LOSE YOUR PURSE OR WALLET

We've all heard horror stories about fraud that's committed using your name, address, SSN, credit card numbers, etc. Identity theft is the fastest-growing crime in America, striking some 700,000 people from all walks of life. Many of us don't know what to do when this dreadful act occurs. I have first hand knowledge: Unfortunately, my friend's wallet was stolen while she was shopping at a department store and within a week the thief/thieves had ordered an expensive monthly cell phone package, applied for a VISA credit card package, had a credit line approved to buy a Dell computer, received a PIN number from the DMV to change her driver's license and personal record information online! Ouch, that hurts!

Here's some critical information to limit the damage in case this happens to you or someone you know:

Everyone always advises, cancel your credit cards immediately, but the key is having the toll free numbers and your card numbers handy so you know who to call. Keep the list where you can find them easily (having to hunt for them is additional stress you WON'T need at that point!). And, you might want to consider exchanging this information with a trusted friend or relative so if you're on the road you can access the information.

File a police report immediately in the jurisdiction where it was stolen. This proves to your credit providers that you were diligent, and is a first step toward an investigation (if there ever is one). Also, get a copy of the report as proof.

But here's what is perhaps most important: Call the three national credit-reporting organizations immediately to place a fraud alert on your name and social security number. Additionally, order credit reports. I had never heard of doing that until advised by a bank that called to talk with me because an application for credit was made over the Internet in my name.

The national credit-reporting organizations' numbers are: Equifax :1-800 525-6285; Experian (formerly TRW): 1-800-301-7195; TransUnion: 1-800-680-7289; Social Security Administration also has a fraud line at 1-800-269-0271.

The alert means any company that checks your credit knows instantly that your information was stolen and they have to contact you by phone to authorize any new credit. By the time my friend did it - almost two weeks after the theft - all the damage had been done (there are records of all the credit checks initiated by the thieves' purchases, none of which she knew about before placing the alert). Since then, no additional damage has been done, and the thieves threw her Gucci wallet away and someone then turned it in to the police. It seems to have stopped the thieves in their tracks.

CHAPTER THREE
DISPELLING GUN MYTHS

"Courage is contagious
When a brave person takes a stand,
The spines of others
Are often Stiffened"
　　　　　　　- Rev. Billy Graham

You may not be sure whether you want to learn how to shoot a gun, let alone buy one, because you've heard so many stories and statistics that illustrate how guns can be detrimental to you. Many of these so-called facts that are bandied around the media and discussed at cocktail parties are truly false, but are considered accurate, especially by people who are against guns. Myths about weapons can endanger women's safety by scaring them and stopping them from using a highly effective way to protect themselves.

To help you get a broader understanding of the gun issue, the following are the most common myths:

"You're more likely to shoot yourself or a family member than an attacker..."
When Los Angeles real estate broker Donna Foster, who was worried about her personal safety, first heard about my women's gun self-defense seminar, she wildly reacted, "It's a fact, I probably would be shot by my own gun. I heard on TV that a gun owner is 43 times more likely to kill a family member than an intruder. So, why would I want a gun?" This fallacious stance, which has crept into our popular culture is almost certainly one of the most common reasons given why women shy away from learning how to shoot a gun.

Who started this false piece of information and why has it gained so much authenticity? These oft-repeated figures derive from an initial study, "Protection or Peril? An Analysis of Firearms-Related Deaths in the Home," published in a 1966 *New England Journal of Medicine* by Dr. Arthur Kellermann and his colleagues, followed by another two studies, "Suicide in the Home in Relationship to Gun Ownership" (1992) and "Gun Ownership as a Risk Factor in the Home," (1993) and which were bank-rolled by the antigun National Center for Policy Analysis (NPIC), Centers for Disease Control (CDC).

The latter study centered on gun-related deaths in the homes in King County (Seattle), Washington. It was limited to fatalities in the home involving a gun which belonged in the home, and found 1.3 accidental deaths, 4.6 criminal homicides and 37 suicides involving firearms. The authors originally warned that the study was of a single nonrepresentative county. To say the least! Both the case studies and control groups in this study had exceptionally high incidences of social dysfunction and instability, including a high incidence of financial instability. For example, 52.7% of case subjects had a history of a household member being arrested; 24.8% had alcohol-related problems; 31.3% had a household history of illegal drug abuse; 31.8% had a household member hit or hurt in a family fight, and 17.3% had a family member hurt so severely in a family fight that medical attention was required.

The authors freely used the "43" as if it were definitive and national even though the case and control groups did not even represent the diversity of the counties studied, let alone a "normal" American family. Also, the researchers acknowledged no attempt was made to count "cases in which burglars or intruders are wounded or frightened away" by defensive gun use, yet concluded that "the advisability of keeping firearms in the home for protection must be questioned."

Furthermore, to prove their hypothesis, Kellermann and his associates assumed that the victim of the crime and the victim of the homicide were the same person. Actually, the deceased may have been the attacker. Indeed, Kellermann says, "Fifteen victims were killed under legally excusable circumstances. Four were shot by police acting in the line of duty."

According to author and attorney Don Kates, "The data presented does not show that even one homicide victim was killed with a gun ordinarily kept in that household. Indeed, the indirect evidence indicates that most of the homicide victims in the study were killed using guns not kept in the victim's home."

Ultimately, it was shown that no more than 4% of the gun deaths in the study could be attributed to the homeowner's gun.

Through the years, peer-reviewers, medical doctors and scholars asked the CDC and Kellermann for the research to evaluate the conclusions. Kellermann steadfastly refused to divulge the raw data for scientific inquiry, which is routinely expected of honest researchers. That naturally raised the question of the validity of any and all of Kellermann's data. Complaints were issued to both the CDC and to members of Congress. In any event, the media continued to spout the spurious "43" implanting it deeper into culture as "scientific proof."

In Spring, 1966, Congressional subcommittee hearings on CDC funding were held and naturally, Kellermann's work was discussed and the CDC's long neglected duties of scientifically scrutinizing his study. One of those who gave testimony during the hearing was Dr. Miguel Faria, Jr., a consultant neurosurgeon and the editor-in-chief of *The Medical Sentinel*—the official publication of the Association of American Physicians and Surgeons. Faria condemned the CDC's abandonment of integrity in research and said, "...when it comes to the NCIPC, we don't have science... You don't go about in science to make a statement and then find corroborative evidence to support that statement...You go the other way around. You gather facts, you test those facts, and then you make a generalization."

Kellermann's study was considered so flawed, the CDC

was forced, finally, to rein in Kellermann. And so, in the summer of 1996, the U.S. House of Representatives voted to shift $2.6 million away from the NCIP of the CDC, earmarking "gun funds" for other health research.

But, Kellermann didn't leave the government dole. Almost immediately after leaving the CDC umbrella, he was picked up by the U.S. Department of Justice's National Institute for Justice (NIJ). It publishes a series of monographs available to the public and the new title of the June 1996 issue was "Understanding and Preventing Violence: A Public Health Perspective," which was a reiteration of Kellermann's past discredited research.

The truth is that 2 million people a year use a gun for self-defense and that 98% of the time the gun is merely brandished to stop a crime. In less than 1% of the cases is a gun actually fired at the attacker. These statistics, researched by John Lott in his seminal book, *More Guns, Less Crime: Understanding Crime and Gun Control Law,* (University of Chicago Press, 2000), received far less media attention and the research was actually derided by critics, who continued to utilize Kellermann's study as the bible of gun facts.

"Why should I own a gun since friends, acquaintances and relatives are the most likely killers."

There is really no broad definition of "acquaintance" used in the FBI's Uniform Crime Reports, and most victims are indeed classified by the FBI as knowing their killer. According to Guy Smith in *Gun Facts,* what's not made clear is that acquaintance murder primarily includes drug buyers killing pushers, cabdrivers killed by their clients, gang members killing other gang members, etc. Only one U.S. city, Chicago, reports a precise breakdown on the nature of acquaintance killings, and the statistics give a very different impression: between 1990 and 1995, just 17% of murder victims were either family members, friends, neighbors or roommates of their killers. The rest

were people with criminal records, killed by other criminals.

"Guns are not effective in preventing crime against women."

Of the 2.5 million annual self defense cases using guns,
more than 7.7% (192,500) are by women defending
themselves against sexual abuse. According to the U.S.
Department of Justice (1998), the probability of serious
injury from an attack is 2.5 times greater for women offer-
ing no resistance than with a gun. As mentioned earlier,
the governmental agency also reports that 27% of women
keep a gun in the house and 37.6 million females either
own or have rapid access to guns.

"I don't want a gun in the house. More children are hurt with guns than any other method."

Women are naturally very worried about guns in the
home, and although some women would consider having a
gun, they tend to be adamant about not having one because they're fearful their children would get a hold of it.
Most people don't realize that very few children are involved in gun deaths.

The National Safety Council (1997) reports that 0.1% of
all deaths for children in the U.S. between 0-14 are from
firearms. The rate of "children" 0-24 years old is 0.4%. In
another study, the National Center for Health Statistics,
National Vital Statistics Report (1997) says that children are
12 times more likely to die in a car accident than from gun-
related homicides or legal interventions (being shot by a
police officer, for example) if they are aged 0-14. For the
group 0-24 years old (which bends the definition of "child")
the rate is still 8.6 times higher for cars.

"Guns are safer when they're locked up."

It's usually assumed that safe storage gun laws reduce
accidental gun deaths and total suicides. According to a

study, *Safe-Storage Gun Laws: Accidental Deaths, Suicide and Crime,* which analyzed both state and county data spanning nearly twenty years, the researchers found no support that these laws reduce either juvenile accidental gun deaths or suicides. "Instead," according to John R. Lott, Jr., the study's lead author, "these storage requirements appear to impair people's ability to use guns defensively. During the first five full years after the passage of the safe storage laws, the group of fifteen states that adopted these laws faced an annual average increase of over 300 more murders, 3,860 more rapes, 24,650 more robberies, and over 25,000 more aggravated assaults."

Lott cites the example of a Merced, California family, whose guns were put away because of the state's safe storage law. The father, John Carpenter, who lost two children in an attack in 2000, said a gun would have stopped the man who broke into his home with a pitchfork. "If a gun had been here, today I'd have at least a daughter alive," Carpenter said.

Although I am not opposed to securing guns, I think it's important to assess your family situation especially if you have children at home and make a determination whether you can educate and trust your children about not handling a gun. In the next chapter, I discuss the issue of children and guns in the home.

"The U.S. has the highest homicide rate in the world because Americans own so many guns."

The Swiss, Finns and New Zealanders have a high gun ownership rate. Switzerland has extremely lenient gun control (more so than U.S.) and has the third lowest homicide rate of the top nine major European countries and the same per capita rate as England and Wales. New Zealand has a lower rate than Australia where guns have been banned. Finland and Sweden have very different gun ownership rates, but very similar homicide rates. Israel, with a higher gun ownership rate than America, has a murder rate 40% lower than Canada. Ironically, many of the countries with the strictest gun control have the highest rates of violent crime. Australia and England which have virtually banned gun ownership have the highest rates of sexual assault, robbery, and assault with force of the top 17 industrialized countries.

In fact, as recently as July, 2002, the British Home Office reported that the true level of crime in England is as much as 40% higher than official figures show. Surveys of crime levels by several police forces show that up to 6,000 more crimes are being committed every day than the current official national figures suggest. Previously the police have recorded only incidents that were actively pursued. Home Secretary, David Blunket, who according to *The Daily Telegraph*, was shocked with the new figures, ordered the police to record every crime reported so that figures were more accurate. In the past, many minor crimes were overlooked if there were a more serious incident to be dealt with: for instance, a theft following a murder would rarely be counted! *The Daily Telegraph* reported that "some crimes have also not been recorded because the victim withdraws a statement or complaint or because officers thought the offence too trivial to pursue."

"If all law-abiding citizens are allowed to carry concealed handguns, people will end up shooting each other."

Millions of Americans currently hold concealed handgun permits and only one permit holder has ever used a concealed handgun after a traffic accident, and that case was ruled as self-defense. Most violations that lead to permits being revoked involve accidentally carrying a gun into restricted areas, like airports or schools.

"In case something horrible happens I can call 911. The police can protect me and people don't need guns."

The courts have continuously ruled that the police do not

have an obligation to protect **individuals.** In *Warren v. District of Columbia Metropolitan Police Department 444A.2d1* (District of Columbia app. 1981), the court states, "Courts have without exception concluded that when a municipality or other government entity undertakes to furnish police services, it assumes a duty only to the public at large and not to individual members of the community."

Currently, approximately 150,000 police officers are **on duty** at any one time. This includes desk clerks, command sergeants, etc. Since there are about 271,933,702 people in the U.S., there is only one **on duty** cop for every 1,813 people. According to *U.S. News & World Report* (July 17, 1998), 95% of the time the police arrive too late to prevent a crime or arrest the suspect. If you call from a cell phone you are even less likely to get help. In over 90% of cities, technology doesn't give police dispatchers the location of the cell phone caller, making police protection less likely for travelers.

Numerous other gun myths circulate through American society and the media, including the constitutional argument regarding the Second Amendment. You can read further by exploring:

      www.americanselfdefense.com/gunfacts3.pdf

CHAPTER FOUR
GUNS, FAMILY PROTECTION AND KIDS

"Courage is resistance to fear, mastery of fear - not absence of fear."
- Mark Twain

"I'm not sure why I'm here learning how to shoot. I've got two kids at home. I <u>am</u> afraid of an intruder breaking in, but I'm also afraid of a gun in the house—that the kids will get hold of it—yet I want to be able to protect them. It's such a terrible conflict," said Sandra, during my seminar for members and their daughters of a local Junior League.

"Yeah, I feel the same way," chimed in Diana, "my husband wants a gun but I'm not sure I can handle one in the house. How do I know that I'll be able to pull the trigger? I've got a four- year-old son who's into everything. There must be a way to keep a gun safe!"

"Safe guns? Hey, I don't even want my five-year-old playing with toy guns," said Alice.

To be sure, there's lots to think about when you have kids and are also thinking about having a gun in the house for protection. More than half of the seven thousand or so people who've attended my personal safety seminars have been mothers, many whose husbands are frequently away, or single parents in charge of their family's safety. Women are nurturers and care-givers, yet the thought of taking responsibility for having a gun in a house with children or grandchildren is frequently too much for some of them to handle.

I certainly understand their anxiety. But in actuality, their fear and apprehension is often more complex than meets the eye. Not infrequently, it stems from doubt and uncertainty as to their own capacity to act, should the need to use a weapon arise. The "courage quotient," I call it.

The critical question to ask yourself: Do I have what it takes to use a gun if that's the most effective way of protecting my family? Coming up with an answer isn't so easy because the state of mental and emotional preparedness that it takes to actually pull a trigger isn't something any of us, male or female, are born with. Nor does courage mean the absence of fear. Some of the bravest women I know didn't start out that way. They <u>learned</u> to be brave by studying and practicing what do to in emergencies. In most cultures, as we discussed in an earlier chapter, bravery and courage are considered testosterone traits, male qualities: "he's got the guts of a lion," "the courage of a bull," or "that takes balls." Not too often (if ever) do we hear: "now that took ovaries!"

But real courage at its roots, is of course, gender-blind. Not an exclusively male prerogative, it's simply doing what you have to do, in the face of real and sometimes paralyzing fear. And, as with most things in life, happily, it's something you can learn. If you want. It's been my experience that anyone so motivated can develop the **courage** to use a gun to protect themselves and their loved ones from harm. How? Through education and training.

The famed Green Berets, Navy Seals and other distinguished combat operatives didn't just pop out of the womb combat ready. They got that way only through rigorous, disciplined training and education so when it's time to be brave and courageous, they know what to do. They're ready! And you can be ready, too! And the closer the crisis is to what you've been trained for, the more courageous (read: prepared) you will be.

Ask yourself the following questions:
> Have I ever been in a situation with my children when I felt threatened and vulnerable?
> Was I fearful?
> What action did I take?
> Was I successful?
> Did I feel good about what I did or didn't do?
> How did my children react?

If the answers you come up with aren't entirely satisfying, consider the difference if you'd been better prepared and known in advance what action to take to best safeguard yourself and your children from whatever harm you had to confront.

The following is a true story of a maverick woman who was prepared:

Jeanine, a St. Louis mother of two sons, a 13-year-old and eight-year-old, had to confront an intruder alone at 4 a.m. while her husband was away on business. The first sign of trouble was the loud noise that awakened Jeanine, who got out of bed to investigate and found a young man in his early 20's, a total stranger, sitting on the roof of her patio storage cabinet and privacy wall three floors above ground level.

She later recalled, "I realized immediately that he was under the influence of drugs by his incoherent mumbling, glassy eyes and bizarre behavior." She ordered him to leave, told him she was calling the police, then slammed and locked the patio door. She yelled to her kids to lock their bedroom door, and then went directly to her bedroom and called the police and the dispatcher assured her a car was on the way.

Aware of the drugged condition of the tall, husky man, who was over six feet tall and weighed 175 pounds (Jeanine is five-foot-two and weighs 125 pounds), she got her gun. Just as she finished loading her gun, Jeanine heard a crash as the intruder forced open the patio door and entered the living room. She knew the police were on the way, but the crisis had not waited for them to arrive.

She moved down the hall toward the living room.

"I knew I was violating the training doctrine which says to stay put, take up a defensive position, and let the intruder come to you," she explained later. "But I felt compelled to put as much distance between the danger and my kids as I could. I didn't know what was about to happen, but I wanted it to be as far away from them as it could be."

Entering the front room, she faced the man at close range - six to eight feet. "I knew instantly he was already too close! I knew that if I had to fire, it would be necessary to shoot him in the head to be sure of stopping him."

She chambered the first round in her pistol. She flicked the safety off, her finger found the trigger, and she leveled the sights right between the man's eyes.

Jeanine did not say a word; her actions spoke for themselves, with great conviction and persuasion. The man looked at her and the pistol pointed at his head and shouted, "Oh shit!" then turned and fled through the door he had forced open, vaulted over the six foot patio privacy wall, and raced down the stairs.

Jeanine ran to the front door, pistol in hand, watching the man's direction of escape. She provided this additional information and a detailed description of the intruder and his clothing to responding police when they arrived several minutes later. Soon after, the suspect was arrested.

This potentially lethal confrontation came to a happy conclusion. No shots were fired; no one was injured. Incidentally, he was out on bond for a previous offense at the time he committed this crime—another all too common story.

I asked her how she managed to do everything right in the face of such danger, terror, and stress. She said, "It seems like I was on automatic pilot. I knew what to do. In time of emergency you seem to do what you are trained to do without thinking about it. I was never conscious of thinking about what I was doing or intended to do next - I just did it. I was prepared to defend my kids, prepared to shoot if necessary; he could not mistake my resolve. That made it his next move. Fortunately for both of us, he made the right choice - he turned and ran."

I asked if she would recommend every family having a gun. She thought for a moment and said, "No, no, you should only have a gun if you have training and you gotta know that you would pull that trigger. Also, if you've got kids, it's got to be put away so they can't get to it."

Of course, there's always a risk in owning a gun when you have children, just as there is a calculated danger in having sharp knives, cleaning fluids, a medicine chest and even a swimming pool. Any sane, serious, responsible person <u>must</u>, in my opinion, be <u>very</u> concerned about having a gun in the house.

Easy to say, I know, but, as a mother, not so simple to do. Having a gun around for personal protection, sports or hunting is one thing. Keeping it **secure** from inquisitive hands is another. The safest gun, child-wise, is, of course, an unloaded one locked in a safe, which also makes it perfectly useless if you need it in a hurry.

If you've got children around and are considering having a gun for that "just-in-case situation," the fact is, you'll probably need to make some basic changes in your home and life style. But if you're a reasonably responsible adult, the task shouldn't be all that daunting or time-consuming. We're not talking rocket science. The biggest question in most people's minds, and rightfully so, is: "should the gun be loaded or unloaded?" The answer can only be arrived at after a thorough, searching appraisal of all the risks and advantages involved.

From years of thinking about the subject, here is what I've learned:

First, make no mistake— loading a handgun in the face of danger, adrenaline pumping, is no Texas Two-Step. According to police authorities and shooting experts, fear and panic render hands and fingers, not to mention arms and legs, and brain, a lot less dependable.

Doubtful? Place an unloaded gun on a table, and put brass (do <u>not</u> use live ammunition) on the other side of the table. Have a friend give you the go-ahead to load and time you. This will in no way simulate the stress of a real crisis, but you will clearly see how clumsy you can become from the mere pressure of being timed. (If you have a revolver, using a speed-loader can help, but only if you become adept at loading in the dark, under extreme pressure).

Considering these adrenaline-induced constraints that usually create the need to use a gun for self-protection, I've concluded that if you're reasonably confident that you can safely secure your loaded handgun from coming into the wrong hands, you're a whole lot better prepared by keeping it loaded rather than unloaded.

What, you say? Keeping a loaded gun around? How politically incorrect, at the very least! But my function here is to deal with reality, not fantasy, and reality requires candor.

Years ago, while writing Armed & Female, I felt differently and said, "Your gun should be loaded only when you are at home, and if, for example, you come home at night and load your gun and then decide to leave, you should unload it and safely secure it again."

I've changed my opinion. I came to realize that most people simply won't take the time to unload and load their guns. It's too much to expect as a practical matter. Even from responsible people. The best way, as I mentioned before, is to keep it loaded, but secured in a portable safe.

I have not changed my mind about unloading a gun and safely securing it if you're going to be away for an extended period of time and not taking it with you. You wouldn't want your Beretta in the hands of a burglar, who more than likely would sell it on the black market to only God knows who.

You may be surprised to learn that 51 percent of all American households possess at least one firearm, so it's reasonable to assume that many children in this country have been taught gun safety and are coexisting comfortably with the risks and benefits of gun ownership. You may argue that you've heard there are a lot of kids getting killed with their parents' guns, so let's talk about statistics.

According to the Centers for Disease Control and

Prevention (CDC), (whose rabid anti-gun bias although well documented is little known by the general public) overall firearm mortality <u>declined</u> 11 percent between 1993 and 1995, while auto fatalities rose 22 percent. The National Safety Council estimates that in 1995 among children under 5, accidental deaths from guns (including rifles and shotguns) numbered 50. That's right, not 500 or 5,000. Fifty. Among all children under age 15 the number was 200, and a majority were gang-related deaths. While accidental gun deaths are always sad and tragic by comparison, 2,900 children died in motor vehicle crashes, 220 children died from choking, 1,000 died from fires and burns, and 950 from drowning. Hundreds more children die in bicycle accidents each year than die from all types of firearm accidents. They just don't make the Six o'clock News.

Child firearms deaths are usually, but certainly not always, the fault of careless adults. It's people just not giving enough attention to securing their guns. According to a 1993 *Los Angeles Times* poll, 4 in 10 gun owners don't keep their guns locked up. Many hide their guns in

---

Home Is Not The Safest Place For A Child To Be

According to two U.S. studies published in May, 2003, a home is not the safest place for a child to be and it's not because of guns!

The studies done at Cincinnati Children's Hospital Medical Center found that home injuries, though continuing to fall, remain a leading cause of death in children and teens, especially African Americans.

The good news was that the annual rate of accidental deaths in the home fell by 25 percent between 1985 and 1997. But the researchers who used government statistics found that dangers still abounded.

The two research teams found that 2,800 children die each year from unintentional injuries in the home. Between 1985 and 1997, 69 percent of deaths in children and adolescents under the age of 20 were the result of such injuries.

Twice as many black children as white children died accidentally in the home — 7 per 100,000 for blacks as compared to 3.3 per 100,000 for whites.

Children younger than 5 and boys were the most likely to be injured, the studies found. The most common causes of injuries and deaths were fires or burns, drowning or suffocation, poisoning and falls. Falls were the leading cause of injury, accounting for 1.5 million visits to emergency rooms.

inappropriate places.

One woman I know stashes her .38 at the bottom of a laundry basket in the bedroom closet. Another hides hers at the back of a top shelf in the kitchen. Other "secret" hiding places include: inside a boot in a closet, inside a vase, a heating vent, a shoe-box and of course, the ubiquitous under-the-mattress. Then there's the old hollowed-out-book trick. During the day, it's mixed in with other books yet immediately available in an emergency. At night, you can keep it near your bed. The problem is, while some of these "hiding places" might at first glance appear inaccessible to an inquisitive child, don't you believe it! Most kids have a unique knack for finding things in the most-out-of-the-way places.

A few of my students feel comfortable storing their guns in locked night-stands during the day and taking them out at night. One drawback is the possibility of misplacing the key, unless it's always kept in the same place—hidden from everyone. Another problem is that night-stand locks are usually not all that secure and can be easily compromised by a burglar or an inventive child. As to having a loaded gun out on the night-stand, unless, you're on the run or rehearsing for a TV episode of "The Sopranos," I don't recommend it.

There are a plethora of trigger locks on the market. I don't recommend them because they can be taken off rather easily and in an emergency, you need to use your gun immediately. However, if you prefer a trigger lock, only use it on an UNLOADED gun. A trigger lock on a loaded gun is totally unsafe.

Smith & Wesson, for example, provides a Master Lock trigger lock with every gun that's sold. The keyed-lock must be placed behind the trigger so the trigger can't be pulled. The manufacturer expressly warns that the gun should not be loaded while locked. The downside is losing or misplacing the key, or worse, your child getting a hold of it.

So, what's the best way to secure a gun? In my opinion,

storing it <u>loaded</u> in a safe along with other guns, jewelry, valuables, etc. As Lyn Bates, contributing editor of *Women & Guns* magazine says, "The consequences of a poorly designed (or wrongly used) security system can have devastating consequences when the gun is loaded, including your gun may be stolen; you may not be able to get to your gun in time when you need it; you may have an unintentional discharge when locking your gun up; a child may get to the loaded gun, an intruder may get to the loaded gun or you may have difficult accessing it."

If you have only one gun, I recommend a small portable safe (also called "lockboxes," "small gun safes," "minisafes," etc.) especially designed for a gun. There are many available on the market and my favorite is the "GunVault," by GunVault, Inc., which comes in many different sizes. This battery-operated durable safe is made of 16-gauge steel housing and looks very presentable. To open, you slide your fingers among the contoured grooves, locate the correct buttons using the braille-like dots and enter your private security code.

Never use the combination that came from the manufacturer. Select a combination that is simple for you to remember and long enough so that someone won't find it by accident. Also, write it down and hide it somewhere. If your child (or an unauthorized adult) gives it a try, the built-in computer will block access after five wrong attempts.

Another feature is audio feedback as you push the combination or it can be disabled if you want to open it without anyone knowing. The lock also has a "Security Sleep Mode," which will become unresponsive after 5 minutes if someone is "playing" with the key pad. A low battery warning tells you when it's time to replace the batteries. I recommend that you get new batteries every six months. (It can also be powered externally if you don't like to use batteries.)

The safe mounts vertically or upside-down, so you can

have it under your bed for easy access without the lid popping open and the gun falling out. Also, all of the GunVaults can be fitted with an optional steel security cable, so that it can be attached to anything around your home, office, car, RV, etc. List prices range from $190 to $240.

Mossberg InstantAccess has a lighted numeric keypad on top. It has two batteries—a main 9 volt one outside the safe, and a backup 9 volt one inside the safe. Either battery will power the lock and a audible signal tells you when either is low. It can be mounted or carried around and comes with a carrying case that doesn't look like a lockbox. List price is $219 and $229 for a marbleized finish.

There are many other lockboxes including one of the first ever made, the Cannon Safe Quicksafe, as well as the PistolPal, the HANDGUN BOX and the V-Line.

When it comes to child gun safety laws, more than a dozen states have enacted Child Access Prevention Laws, (CAP), a.k.a. "safe storage" laws, that require adults to either store loaded guns in a place that is reasonably inaccessible to children, or use a device to lock the gun. If a child obtains an improperly stored, loaded gun, the adult owner is criminally liable. Some states require gun stores to provide purchasers with a written notice about the law, and to place a warning sign at the counter.

Chicago was the first city to <u>mandate</u> the use of trigger locks and the police can now go house to house and arrest

States with CAP Laws:
California
Connecticut
Delaware
Florida
Hawaii
Iowa
Maryland
Massachusetts
Minnesota
Nevada
New Jersey
North Carolina
Rhode Island
Texas
Virginia
Wisconsin

Some cities have made it a crime to leave a loaded firearm where children can access it:
Elgin and Aurora, Illinois
Houston, Texas
Baltimore, Maryland

owners who don't have them on their guns and confiscate their firearms!

Massachusetts was the first state to require that all guns sold in the state come equipped with a lock. It's unclear how the state will enforce the regulation. Will they also go house to house with search warrants? It seems that there are a number of show-boating politicians out there getting ready for the next election. Federal legislators are also looking into adopting similar requirements.

Regrettably, safety rules don't always increase safety. Take the example of "child-resistant" medicine bottle caps. Harvard University economist W. Kip Viscusi claims that these caps result each year in "3,500 <u>additional</u> poisonings of children under age 5 from (aspirin-related drugs). . .(as) consumers have been lulled into a less-safety conscious mode of behavior by the existence of safety caps."

As we discussed before in Chapter 2, guns clearly deter criminals. Polls by the *Los Angeles Times*, Gallup and Peter Hart Research Associates show that there as few as 760,000, and as many as 3.6 million, defensive uses of guns occur each year.

The defensive nature of guns is further revealed in the different rates of so-called "hot burglaries," those where a victim is at home when a burglar strikes. In Canada and Britain which both have tough very restrictive gun-control laws, almost half of all burglaries are "hot." In America, where greater gun ownership is permissible, only 13% of burglaries are "hot." Criminals don't behave differently simply by chance. U.S. felons admit in surveys that when committing crimes they are much more worried about encountering an armed victim than about the police.

In my opinion, it makes more sense to support the prosecution of those adults whose careless behavior results in an avoidable death or serious injury than to limit the rights of law abiding citizens to protect and defend themselves against criminal invasions.

A FAMILY CODE SYSTEM

If you're planning to have a gun in your home and family members from time to time come home at night after you've gone to bed, I strongly recommend that you establish a code system so you will **never, ever** mistake your child or significant other for an intruder. Let's say that your teenager returns home at midnight. Rather than being quiet and tiptoeing in when entering, they should be instructed to awaken you and call out a code word or phrase you've agreed upon in advance. Following this simple procedure can help avoid confusion when you're awakened by footsteps or noise.

SHOOTING AND PREGNANCY: DO THEY MIX?

Over the years, I've received many calls from pregnant women asking if the sounds of gunfire can be transmitted into the uterus and hurt the fetus's hearing? Should prospective mothers take precautions against exposure to lead fumes? Also, is it safe for a pregnant woman to clean a gun?

According to obstetrician and gynecologist, Dr. Curtis Vickers, fetal ear development begins between the 8th and 10th weeks of pregnancy. He says the womb environment is cushioned against exterior influences. "Some sound waves will transmit through," he explains in *Women & Guns* magazine, (August, 1995) "It's simple physics that sound transmits best through solids, second-best through liquids. Sound's worst transmission is through air. Wherever you have an interface you lose some of that transmission. So sounds traveling through air and then hitting skin—which is considered a fluid medium—and then all the body's layers to the fetus, it's doubtful that the sound waves generated by most guns would cause any problems."

And what about lead exposure from discharged rounds? There haven't been any definitive studies on pregnancy and exposure to lead at an indoor gun range. However, many studies describe the amount of lead exposure in numerous range settings and consequences of the amount of lead exposure to the fetus during pregnancy. We know that developing fetuses are extraordinarily sensitive to lead—more so than children and far more so than adults.

According to Dr. John M. Latz, "In children, blood lead levels as low as 10 micrograms/deciliter of blood causes damage. In adults, lead levels must reach 4—50 micrograms/deciliter to produce symptoms. Therefore, the danger is that while the adult may feel fine at a level of 10, 20 or 30 micrograms/deciliters, the developing fetus may be irreparably harmed given that children experience damage at 10 micrograms/deciliter. Remember, also, that lead does cross the placenta into the fetus's circulation and also is found in breast milk."

Does this all mean no shooting while pregnant? Dr. Latz contends that if you do shoot, adequate range ventilation is necessary and you should monitor your blood levels. He advises that you consult with your physician. My attitude about pregnancy and shooting? Why take the chance. If you want to practice, "dry-fire" (that means no bullets!) at home.

TOY GUNS

What about toy guns? Should you allow your kids to play with them? It's a matter of personal choice. When my sons were tots, I never gave them toy guns, but when they turned seven and eight, my husband, returning after a long business felt a necessity to buy them plastic rifles. I protested, but they were already playing with them.

Today, I see very obvious ill effects from kids playing with toy guns. To me, guns are tools, not toys. In my mind, a **toy gun** is an oxymoron. In today's violence-filled world, children see guns grievously misused and mishandled daily on T.V., in video games, and in far too many instances, in real life. Such exposures coupled with allowing play with toy guns just further confuses children as to guns, their function and the harm they can do. In 1997, Toys 'R' Us took toy guns off their shelves. (Management claimed they were not selling well). As far as I'm concerned, taking toy guns off the market would be a very effective means of helping dispel the confusion. Without toy guns, whenever a kid saw a gun, they'd know it is real. And nothing to be played around with.

GUN-PROOFING YOUR CHILDREN

Having safely locked your gun away, can you now sit back secure in the knowledge that you've done everything possible to avert an accident? The answer is no. There is no way to 100% child-proof your guns, unless you also gun-proof your children. What am I talking about? And just how and when do you undertake the task?

There is certainly no possibility of a baby in a crib finding a loaded gun, so you've got maybe a year to think about it. According to the National Safety Council, the number of infants killed, accidentally or criminally (usually child abuse!) with firearms is on the order of only 10 out of nearly 40,000 such gun deaths. They don't call it the *terrible twos* for nothing, because between the ages of two and four, nothing is safe in the house from those curious little hands.

So as soon as there is comprehension, start making it clear to your youngsters that they are NEVER, EVER, NEVER to touch, handle or remain in the presence of a gun, at home or anywhere else, unless you are personally there with them. If they're at a friend's house and a gun is present, they should leave the house immediately and tell you about it when they get home.

After you're certain that message has been communicated loud and clear, as and when the child is old enough and interested, you can advance the child-proofing process by incorporating all the do's and don't's of safe and responsible gun handling as a positive parent-child bonding activity.

The ideal strategy is to show a child how your gun

operates while you're cleaning it, and then, later, to take them to a range and show them what really happens when the trigger is pulled. Once a child understands how a gun operates, has heard the sound and fury of a gunshot, up close, and witnessed the damage a gun can do, he or she will have a vastly different view of a gun along with a newfound sense of respect and caution.

At what age should children be educated about guns? There is really no hard and fast rule, but one good barometer may be evidenced in the care of the family pet. A child mature enough to responsibly handle the feeding, medication, and cleaning chores of a household pet is generally old enough to be taught how to be trustworthy with guns. Of course, there are some children (as well as some adults), who, no matter how old, are emotionally unstable and should never handle a gun.

When you believe your child is mature enough to see what really happens when a gun is shot, take them to an outdoor range or other outdoor safe area and try the following exercise, which in my opinion, graphically and dramatically gets the point across.

After making certain your child is comfortably equipped with appropriate eye and ear protection, set a cantaloupe or other melon on a box about seven yards away. Then stand back with the child and have them watch as you fire a round (preferably a hollow point, because it is more damaging) into the melon exploding it off the mark! With your child, examine the incredible destruction and locate where the bullet entered and exited. Since a melon is quite similar in size to a human head, you can easily explain the kind of damage that would occur if a person were shot with just one bullet. I cannot emphasize enough how critical this lesson is to your child's true understanding of guns. Most kids think a bullet only makes a small hole in the body, like the thousand or more they see every year on T.V. Your youngster may be frightened after this exercise, but if it takes a little fear to gain respect for a gun, it is well worth the effort.

If and when you think your children are ready to shoot, your next step is some kind of proper instruction. You can, of course, do your own teaching. You might also consider contacting a local NRA club that offers firearms familiarization programs. Also, give them the NRA's "Eddie Eagle" training about firearms. Their message is "if you see a gun, don't touch it, leave the area immediately, tell an adult." Junior Rifle courses afford nonathletic kids an excellent way to learn the meaning of teamwork and the excitement of competition.

Your kids don't necessarily have to be target shooters in order for you to gun-proof them. What they need to know, through your own gun-safety practice and instruction, is that guns are <u>dangerous</u> and must be treated with great respect. If they learn that, your concern will not be that your child may take your gun, but that your son or daughter may be in another child's home and that an irresponsible child may take the family gun our of a drawer or a closet.

KIDS & GUN SELF DEFENSE

I also recommend that at a certain age your daughters and sons join a martial arts or kick boxing class, but they should also take a gun self-defense course. I remember one mother, Barbara, a Ketchum, Idaho mother of three daughters, took my seminar, and called me that evening saying she wanted to enroll her three daughters in my next seminar that following weekend. She said she was so excited about her new feeling of empowerment, she wanted to pass on that experience to her daughters. "My youngest is eleven," she explained, "and I especially want her to know that she has control over her body, in fact, her life, and that she can defend herself."

I'll never forget that Sunday when all three sisters were on the shooting line having the time of their lives. And guess who shot the best? The youngest who was eleven years old! She was a better marks-woman than any of the adults. When I asked her how she felt, she said in her eleven year-old style, "this is very cool."

KIDS & COMPETITIVE SHOOTING

According to the National Shooting Sports Foundation (NSSF) spokesman Gary Mehalik, more and more kids are seeking an alternative to traditional after-school sports and turning to competitive shotgun shooting with NSSF's Scholastic Clay Target Program (ages 6-12) for an experience they claim "unmatched on any playing field." Even the Brady Campaign to Prevent Gun spokesperson Nancy Hwa says, "We don't have a problem with target shooting and sport shooting. But we do think that parents have to be very careful about the maturity level of their children, about how the guns are being handled."

Accident prevention is the top priority. No training is conducted on school grounds. Once the kids have demonstrated their "maturity and sense of responsibility," they start their competitive training at their local firing range.   Competitive shooters who show outstanding marksmanship are invited to participate in NSSF's Junior Olympic Training Development Camp in Colorado Springs, CO, which provides an opportunity for young women and men to hone their skills with top Olympic shotgun coaches as well as a place to display their talents for future consideration on the U.S. team. (See Chapter 8 for more information).

Whatever decision you make in regards to having a gun at home, remember, as a responsible adult, make absolutely certain that your gun is safely secured so your children and their friends will not handle them unless you want them to. As far as your children are concerned, gun safety is <u>your</u> responsibility!

CHAPTER FIVE
WHAT GUN SHOULD I BUY?

Baton Rouge, LA, July 31, 2002 — Police in the Louisiana capital were searching for a suspected serial killer on Wednesday after DNA tests linked one man to the brutal murders of three women in the past 10 months. Local authorities warned women to take precautions, but had little information to offer them about the killer or what he looked like. Louisiana Governor Mike Foster reminded women Thursday that they can pack a gun to protect them from a serial killer. "You have the right to get a gun permit," Foster said, "Learn to use it."

First of all, you can't buy a handgun on the internet! Even on *Ebay* it's off limits. You can purchase a gun at a gun store, a gun show or from another person. But, every state has different laws regarding purchasing a gun, so learn the rules by going online to the National Rifle Association website.

If you want to buy a gun for self defense, don't purchase one until you've taken a gun safety and training course. First, you need to feel comfortable shooting a gun and most importantly, you need to know that you could shoot someone who is attacking you or a loved one. I have met a number of women who clearly said they could not shoot anyone even if he was a bad person, intending grave physical harm to them or their children. I've always replied, "then, you shouldn't own a gun."

Brandishing a gun at someone doesn't always stop him. The truth is if you point a gun at an attacker and don't intend to shoot him and you hesitate, he'll sense it and come after you. He could easily grab the gun away from you and kill you.

Once you've taken some classes, you'll begin to understand who you are in terms of your fears, personal convictions, mental readiness and physical abilities. In my Empowerment Seminars, after my introductory remarks, each woman briefly tells the class why she's there. All of them voice their concerns about crime and their personal safety and want to know how to take care of themselves. But nearly all are scared about learning how to shoot a gun and some are nervous about having one in the house.

I remember a woman named Alana, a 32 year old spirited, high-powered advertising agency executive, who was quite candid about guns. "I don't want to be here. I don't like guns and I'm frightened of guns. My husband owns lots of guns and they're in the house and I won't touch them. He wants me to learn how to use them just in case he's not home," explained Alana. "He drove me here and literally pushed me through the door," joked Alana, laughing at herself.

Although Alana is a large-boned woman with big hands and could easily hold a .357 Magnum, she insisted that she learn on a "small gun." She was so terrified of guns that the thought of handling a large-framed gun was too scary for her. Even holding an unloaded snubbed-nosed .38 special in the classroom made her anxious. She re-marked to everyone that she was sure that she would "shoot her toes off."

Alana was also worried about the gun's recoil. She called it "the kick," and heard that she could be knocked off her feet by "the kick." Like so many of my students, Alana was a real challenge to me. Frankly, while I in-structed her in the classroom with my marvelous friends and assistants, Phyliss and Fred Cook, I was concerned that she wouldn't be able to do live-fire shooting on the range. She seemed so confused and had a hard time remembering how to unload the revolver. To help her, my assistant, Phyllis, took her aside and worked with her for about 15 minutes until she finally was at ease with the mechanics of holding a gun. (I'll tell you later what happened to her once she started shooting).

Her dread of the gun plus her apprehension that she couldn't control a handgun is typical of many first-time shooters. Control is a major issue for women because they believe that they won't be able to safely handle a firearm.

As a gun instructor, I have to reassure the students that they are all capable of handling and shooting a gun.

Over the last 11 years, I have taught seminars in rural, suburban and urban areas throughout the US and I continually hear women's stories of why they a fear gun, often to the point of being phobic. But, at least the women who take my all-day course have made some commitment and are open to conquering their fears.

Based on my experience, I have found it much simpler to teach beginning shooters how to shoot revolvers rather than semiautomatic (also called auto-loaders) pistols. It's not that I'm against semi-autos (I own a few and I enjoy shooting them), but they are more complicated to operate than "wheel guns." A novice shooter finds it difficult to load a magazine, especially if she has long manicured fingernails or has arthritis. Because women are usually not as strong as men, a woman often has difficulty thrusting the magazine forcefully enough into the magazine well to ensure a good seating. Often, too, she may have trouble pulling back the slide and then releasing it smoothly.

Also, it's far easier to see if a revolver is loaded or unloaded. With a pistol, to visually verify if a cartridge is in the firing chamber, you need to do a pinch-check. Again, this is not a simple task for a first-time shooter.

If the semi-auto has a de-cocking lever or a safety, learning how to manipulate it quickly and successfully is not easy for a beginner. I have frequently watched a novice shooter forget to release the safety before shooting. Her inability to recover immediately often leaves her feeling anxious that she can't control the firearm. She then believes the firearm controls her.

Furthermore, if a semi-auto malfunctions, it isn't an effortless procedure to clear the stoppage. It takes practice—a lot of practice! (I can't tell you how many times, I've practiced clearing a "double-feed" and a "stove-pipe"). A number of lightning-fast steps have to be completed in just the right order to fire a cartridge, eject the empty case, recock the hammer, and chamber a new round. Also, when I've explained to a beginner that her pistol may malfunction, often, she panics, and loses confidence that she can't control the gun.

In a semiautomatic pistol class that I taught in Spokane, Washington, I heard a student cry out, "Malfunction! Is it going to blow up in my face?" "No," I said, but it wasn't easy to convince her that it wouldn't happen.

Another factor that can't be ignored is that it's simpler to clean and dismantle a revolver, and everyone should know that after you've shot your gun you need to clean it. Even though a semiautomatic will come with instructions in the manufacturer's box showing how to break down the gun, it's not easy to follow the instructions. Disassembling a semi-auto requires some dexterity and strength, especially when replacing the slide. The best way to learn is to have someone show you how to do it and then practice over and over again.

Finally, and unfortunately, many gun owners—female or male—don't target practice. They simply put their guns away in a safe, in a drawer, or underneath their pillow. And when they finally go out to practice, some people don't

---

CLEANING YOUR GUN

There are many different gun cleaners on the market, but my favorite is M-Pro 7, which is non-toxic, biodegradable and odorless. Users include the U.S. Air Force, Army, and Marine Corps, the Los Angeles County Sheriff's Department, Missouri Police Department, Canadian Military, Japanese Military, etc.

Before you clean your gun with M-Pro 7, always make sure the revolver or semi-auto is unloaded and disassembled according to manufacturers' instructions. Spray the cleaner on the entire firearm and brush with a nylon brush to remove exterior carbon deposits. Wipe down with a dry cloth (use cotton swabs for hard to reach areas) and re-oil to protect the finish.

Bore: To clean the bore, swab with a patch thoroughly soaked with gun cleaner. Wait 1-5 minutes and then run a bore brush through the full length of the barrel 2 or 3 times. Run a dry cleaning patch down the bore. Continue applying patches soaked with gun cleaner followed by dry cleaning patches until the patches are white.

remember how to safely handle a gun. At least when they own a revolver it's less complicated to load, shoot and unload it.

Couple all of the above considerations with a novice shooter's "fear factor," and it makes sense for a woman (and for that matter, a man) to learn how to shoot a revolver rather than a semi-auto. Of course, once you feel competent with a revolver, and if you want to learn how to shoot a semi-auto, you'll find that since you've gained confidence around a revolver, it will be easier to learn how to shoot a 9mm, a .45 or .40 semiautomatic.

Those who have learned on a revolver and are interested in a semiautomatic may want to try the Smith & Wesson Model 3953, a 9mm double-action-only pistol with no de-cocking lever. This is a good choice for those transitioning from a revolver to a pistol. The double-action-only function requires the trigger be pulled through the complete firing cycle, which is similar to a revolver being shot in double action.

POSTSCRIPT

You may have wondered how Alana fared in shooting that day. Well, she quickly moved up to a .357 Magnum, with a 4-inch barrel. And, she was the best and the fastest shooter in the class! At the end of the day when we returned to the classroom for graduation, Alana, who was all pumped up, announced to everyone that she lost her fear.

"I love shooting! I love the gun I used! I want to take it up as a sport! I can't wait to show my husband my target," Alana gleefully said.

The entire class broke into applause and cheered her.

Soon after, Alana and her husband decided to do competition shooting and joined an IPSC (International Practical Shooting Confederation) club, which involves shooting a number of scenarios, that use targets that are about the size of the head and upper torso of a person.

IPSC trains you to reload quickly, to run safely from one

place to another with a gun in your hand, and to shoot at targets that are moving or partially hidden.

The last I heard from Alana she was beginning to place first, beating her husband!

AMMUNITION

Ammunition manufactured in the United States is among the best in the world. For self-defense use, select ammunition produced by the most widely recognized manufacturers. These include Cor-Bon, Federal, Remington and Winchester. I don't recommend ammunition that is hand loaded, re-loaded, or of foreign manufacture for **defensive** rounds.

Ammunition is expensive, especially for the larger calibers such as a .45-caliber. So, when you're **practicing**, purchase "target loads" or reloads and have high-quality ammo in your gun when you are at home or traveling. Target loads are usually called wadcutters or semi-wadcutters. The bullet is square in front.

In the past, most ballistic experts recommended hollow-point bullets for self defense. Hollow-point bullets are hollow from the leading edge of the bullet back almost to where the brass case encloses it. The hollow-point bullet is designed to spread and more than double its size after it enters the human body. It has excellent stopping power because it wreaks such enormous damage, and is less likely to pass through your target and endanger someone else. Hollow-points tend to ricochet less than standard bullets, which minimizes the likelihood of wounding an innocent bystander who may be within range.

Bullet selection for an autoloader is much more critical than for a revolver because autoloaders are designed to use smooth, round bullets so they won't get snagged on the way to the chamber. For the autoloader, hollow-points have been designed with a metal jacket surrounding the hollow-point bullet.

Also, there's a new type of ammo called "frangible" ammunition, which is revolutionary and is available to citizens through Bismuth Cartridge, Hevi-Shot, Longbow, Precision Ammunition and PMC. It is **lead-free so it's environmentally safe** and it comes in all calibers except .22 ammo. "Frangible" means fragile, breakable and capable of fracturing into tiny fragments when it hits a surface that is harder than it is. That means there are no ricochets or back splatter. Nonetheless, since it is "round-nosed," it will go through the walls of a typical home or apartment and could hit a family member or a neighbor. You can use this ammo for practice on all ranges—indoor and outside. It's expensive, but the benefit to your health, the environment and the safety of innocent people is immeasurable.

MY FAVORITE GUNS:

I've always thought of a gun as analogous to a shoe: what fits me and is comfortable for me, may not be the same for someone else. After saying this, I do have some favorite handguns that you may want to rent and shoot before deciding what to purchase.

Favorite Revolvers:

My all-around favorite revolver for home self-defense is the stainless steel Smith & Wesson Model 65, four inch barrel, chambered for the .357 Magnum, although I practice with .38 loads.

For carrying concealed, I like a Smith & Wesson Model 64 with its concealed hammer, which lessens the chances of it snagging on something.

Favorite Semi-Automatics:

My favorite 9mm semi-automatic is a P26 Sig Sauer; it has never malfunctioned on me! I also like the classic .45 caliber, 1911 light-weight Colt Commander.

For carrying concealed, I prefer a .380 Sig Sauer, Model P230. It, too, has never jammed on me.

Another 9mm semi-automatic that I like is a Beretta Cougar, Model 8000L; it's short, but not too short!

Another good semi-auto for carrying concealed is the .380 caliber Beretta Model 86FS Cheetah. The barrel can be tipped up by flipping a lever, allowing it to be immediately loaded one round at a time in an emergency and allows a user to load the pistol without having to retract the slide.

Paxton Quigley's Photograph Section

Left:
Paxton teaching at Long Beach Shooting Range (Long Beach, California.)

Below:
Students at Orange County Shooting and Training Center (Tustin, California)

Right:
Paxton on the set of Walker Texas Ranger with Chuck Norris

Bottom:
At a Smith & Wesson event at Sports Unlimited (Louisville, Kentucky)

Top:
Paxton teaching a student (Ketchum, Idaho)

Left:
Photo Flier for Paxton's Seminar (Tucson, Arizona)

You Are Invited To Attend A Woman's Seminar

Women's Empowerment In The 90's

Presented By
PAXTON QUIGLEY

"Twelve million women are gun owners, and they're finding a guru named Paxton Quigley. Her message is being heard."
Tom Brokaw, "NBC Nightly News"

Paxton Quigley (Left) is the author of ARMED & FEMALE and NOT AN EASY TARGET. She has taught thousands of women personal safety strategies. She has appeared on more than 300 radio & t.v. shows and have been widely quoted in major newspapers and women's magazines, including THE WALL STREET JOURNAL, GLAMOUR MAGAZINE, TODAY SHOW and 60 MINUTES.

THE PERSONAL SAFETY & AWARENESS STRATEGIES SEMINAR WILL TEACH YOU:

Awareness Techniques: Most Attacks Can Be Avoided.
Psychological Profiles of Attackers: Who Do They Look For? Are You A Target?
How To Avoid: Follow-Homes, Street Robberies, Car Hi-Jackings, and Other Daylight Attacks.
Security Tips In The Home, Verbal & Physical Self-Defense, Non-Lethal Sprays & Other Self-Defense Weapons.
Handguns: Gun Safe Handling, Rules & Laws, Legal, Moral & Ethical Responsibilities.
Overcoming Women's Culturally Conditioned Fear Of Guns.
Shooting Proficiency: Classroom Training & Range Target Exercises, Including: Prone Shooting,
Point Shooting, One-Handed Shooting & Moving & Shooting.

JENSEN'S, 5146 Pima, Tucson

BEGINNER SEMINAR: SUNDAY, OCTOBER, 19TH, 10-4pm

SEMINAR TUITION: $150 RANGE FEE (paid that day): $24

For Information & Reservations: Diane, 520-325-3346

Make checks For $150 Payable To: Paxton Quigley Enterprises, Inc.

Top:
Paxton teaching students how to yell in Atlanta, Georgia.
Bottom:
Shooting from a prone position, Long Beach Firing Range,
Long beach, California.

Top:
Paxton teaching students at LAX Firing Range in Los Angeles, California.
Bottom:
Paxton teaching a student how to clean a gun.

CHAPTER SIX
YOU AND YOUR GUN

"If someone comes to kill you, arise quickly and <u>kill</u> him."
- The Talmud, Tractate Sanhedrin. 1994. The Schottenstein Edition. New
York: Mesorah Publications. Vol. 2, 72a.

One of the most common questions I'm asked is "what gun do I recommend for a woman?" Unfortunately, there's no easy answer. Often, finding the right gun for yourself takes trial and error and you probably should rent (by the way, renting is not an option in New York) many different models at gun ranges before purchasing one. I always explain that a gun is like a shoe; what's "comfortable" for me may not be "comfortable" for you. A comfortable gun is one that fits your hand and you can shoot it as accurately as possible. Also, knowing how to clean it and fix the gun, if it malfunctions is part of your comfort level. You should never fear your gun. It should become one of your best friends in case you need it for self-protection. Additionally, if you like to sport-shoot and you're single, you've got a built-in hobby where you could meet your soul-mate—remember girls, a lot of guys—doctors, lawyers, teachers, professionals, businessmen, you name it—enjoy going to the shooting range.

And as I said before, probably the most important issue is could you shoot your attacker? I've spoken to a number of women who have told me that even if their lives were in danger, they could not shoot anyone. My reply to them is simple: don't think of it as shooting the assailant, but rather **stopping** him from inflicting harm against you. It is not to kill or wound him.

THE PSYCHOLOGY OF STOPPING YOUR ATTACKER OR AT-TACKERS

To survive on the street or in your home, you want to prevent a potential aggressor from assaulting you or get him to stop the attack. For some people to get to that step is difficult either for religious reasons, political affiliation, psychological upbringing, media information, or a combination of all of them. It also means getting over "the fear factor."

A number of self defense experts have written magazine articles about being psychologically prepared to stop an attacker. A common recommendation is getting training so that you can be psychologically ready to achieve that "Stopping" state of mind. And it turns out, **trained** individuals are far more successful in an actual self defense experience than those who are untrained. Prepared people usually survive.

While reviewing the book, *True Stories of Americans Defending Their Lives With Firearms,* Paul Markel, in *Combat Handguns,* (September 2003), observes that "throughout the ("book") we see that those persons with prior training and experience fared far better and received little or no injury compared to the defender who merely owned a gun."

I have attended the following courses and highly recommend them:

The American Pistol Institute, Jeff Cooper, Paulden, Arizona; Chapman Academy of Practical Shooting, Ray Chapman, Hallsville, Missouri; Lethal Force Institute, Masaad Ayoob, Concord New Hampshire; Defensive Training , Inc., John and Vicky Farnam, Niwot, Colorado; Smith & Wesson Academy, Springfield, Mass. and Executive Security International, Bob Duggan, Rifle, Colorado. (I have also taken courses from Mike Dalton and Mickey Fowler, American Shootist Institute, California, when they worked together and additionally attended the short-lived but terrific, G. Gordon Liddy Academy, G. Gordon Liddy). Although non-gun oriented, I strongly recommend IMPACT, which has the reputation of quickly ridding oneself of the "the fear factor," and has training centers throughout the country. (Classes are for women, children and men).

RESISTING AN ATTACKER

Data from the 1979-1985 installments of the Justice Department's Annual National Crime Victim Survey show that when a woman resists a stranger rape with a gun, the probability of completion was 0.1 percent and of victim injury 0.0 percent, compared to 31 percent and 40 percent, respectively, for all stranger rapes (Kleck, *Social Problems*, 1990).

A paper (Southwick, *Journal of Criminal Justice*, 2000) analyzed victim resistance to violent crimes generally, with robbery, aggravated assault and rape considered together. Women who resisted with a gun were 2.5 times more likely to escape without injury than those who did not resist and 4 times more likely to escape uninjured than those who resisted with any means other than a gun. Similarly, their property losses in a robbery were reduced more than six-fold and almost three-fold, respectively, compared to the other categories of resistance strategy.

Two studies in the last 20 years directly address the outcomes of women who resist attempted rape with a weapon. (Lizotte, *Journal of Quantitative Criminology*, 1986; Kleck, Social Problems, 1990.) The former concludes, "Further, women who resist rape with a gun or knife dramatically decrease their probability of completion." (Lizotte did not analyze victim injuries apart from the rape itself.) The latter concludes that "resistance with a gun or knife is the most effective form of resistance for preventing completion of a rape"; this is accomplished

DOES YOUR GUN FIT YOUR HAND?

Although most of us learn how to shoot a handgun with two hands, in a gun battle hands and arms usually take the first hits. This could leave you with only one hand to shoot your gun, so when selecting your gun, practice shooting it with your dominant hand, as well as your weaker one. Many of the gun manufacturers, such as Smith & Wesson and Beretta are now making guns fit the human hand.

As I mentioned in *Armed & Female*, "The difficulty in selecting a suitable handgun comes in deciding first upon either an autoloader or a revolver, then upon a caliber that will suit your needs, then upon a size of handgun, than upon a grip or stock that can be gripped comfortably and will allow your <u>trigger finger to touch the trigger at the proper place.</u> Fitting these four requirements into one gun is quite a job. *If your gun does not fit you in any of these areas, you will not shoot it well, and that is nearly the same as not having a gun at all."*

Remember, that the longer the barrel, the more accurate the gun will be over seven yards (although most self-defense actions occur within seven yards), and the heavier the gun will be. A heavy handgun is only a detriment if you plan to conceal it in a purse, fanny pack, holster, or will be carrying it in the car.

Also, If you have a tough time reacting to a gun's recoil, find another gun that you can manage. I remember my first revolver, a snub-nosed five-shot revolver, with a recoil that left the "webbing" between my left thumb and second finger (yes, I'm a southpaw!) a bloody, painful mess that needed iodine and a big band-aid. It didn't take me long to sell that gun! One of the best ways to familiarize yourself with your gun is to dry-fire it, although you won't feel the recoil.

When you first learn to shoot or if you only get to the range twice a year, I suggest to my students that they spend at least one half hour a day for two weeks just handling the *unloaded* gun. Again, make sure that your gun is unloaded each time you pick it up. In *Armed & Female*, I recommend that while you are watching television, get to know your gun. "Aim at the TV or at lamps around the room and pull the trigger; pull the slide back and lock it back, if your gun has that feature, then unlock it and slide it forward again—slowly. Never let the slide snap and always let it snap forcefully forward... Switch hands, aim using your sites and fire at the television. Handle your gun as much as you can for the first few days, until it feels like part of your hand and at least one spot on your hand is sore from the unaccustomed contract with the strange piece of metal."

If you plan to legally carry your weapon in a purse, fannypack, holster, etc., first spend time carrying it unloaded in your home, so that you can get the "feel" of the gun. Then at home, practice drawing the unloaded gun from its concealment. As Jeff Cooper, the legendary gun instructor, said to me while I attended his class, "In a gun battle, who ever shoots first has the best chance of winning the fight." Knowing this, drawing the weapon quickly becomes paramount and is often overlooked by the practicing novice shooter.

Also, I recommend that you take a class in handgun retention. As Duane Thomas succinctly explains in *Handguns For Sport & Defense* magazine (October 1992, page 43), "...When you face a violent criminal across your gun's sights, whether he has his own handgun or not, there's always one gun present with which he can kill you if he can get his hands on it—your own!"

Since 1991, Massad Ayoob of the Lethal Force Institute (1-800-624-9049) has been presenting weapon retention training to his entry-level students. (By the way, I highly recommend Ayoob's entertaining, yet serious handgun courses). Another gun self defense school, the Firearms Academy of Seattle (1-800-327-2666), is the only other school in the country that teaches a highly effective weapon retention class to civilians based on the Lindell Method, which was developed in 1975 by James Lindell, an instructor in Defensive Tactics for the Kansas City Regional Police Academy. Many of his maneuvers are based on his background in judo and other martial arts.

WHEN PRACTICING WITH A CARDBOARD SILHOUETTE, WHERE DO YOU SHOOT?

In most beginner classes, you will learn to shoot to the center of mass. In intermediate and expert levels, you will be shooting both to the torso and to the face.

Why to the face? Recently, more "bad guys" are wearing body armor and the only way to stop them is to shoot their face, since the torso is safely covered. It is certainly difficult to shoot to the face because when we think of a face, we can think of it in a spiritual way as well as a physical way. As part of your survival skills, practice and become confident in the head shot for that just in case situation.

CHAPTER SEVEN

SHOULD YOU CARRY A CONCEALED WEAPON?

"I must not fear. Fear is the mind-killer. Fear is the little-death that brings total obliteration. I will face my fear. I will permit it to pass over me and through me. And when it has gone past I will turn the inner eye to see its path. Where the fear has gone there will be nothing. Only I will remain."
- excerpt from "Dune," by Frank Herbert, 1965.

Brenda Barnett, 47, who lives in Hailey, Idaho, a town adjacent to the world famous ski resort, Sun Valley, commutes to Boise for business at least once a week. The three hour trip, mostly on a two-lane highway is almost deserted certain times of the year and is usually a dull drive except Brenda livens it up by listening to "Books on Tape." Halfway through a trip one grey October morning, Brenda looked up at the rear view mirror and saw a fast approaching red pickup truck. As it drew closer to her, she noticed two young men in the vehicle. Thinking nothing of it, she slowed down so the truck could pass her.

"As the truck came alongside me, the guy in the passenger side made some lewd gestures at me, and all of a sudden, the truck bumped the side of my car," Brenda recalled. "I started going faster, but the truck hit me again and I realized they were trying to force me off the road. No one was on the highway and I was scared."

But not scared enough. Brenda picked up her .357 four-inch barrel Taurus which she always keeps on the passenger seat and held it up in the air. "Those guys took one look at that big gun," Brenda laughed, "and they were off like greased lightning."

Brenda has a license to carry a concealed weapon in the state of Idaho and even though the crime rate in Idaho is low compared to other states, she always has her gun in her car or concealed in a purse, ready if something potentially dangerous befalls her.

To many people's surprise, numerous American women not only own their own guns but also legally carry them. For example, in Arizona, out of 67,000 people who legally carry handguns, 6,200 of them are women. Of course, a woman (or a man) should be trained in carrying a gun and shooting from the origin of concealment whether it's a fanny pack, purse, briefcase, jacket pocket, etc.

Antigun critics state that women get a false sense of security when they carry a gun. I disagree; when i have carried a gun I have felt more in control of my surroundings and certainly far safer. I have spoken to countless women, who legally carry concealed guns and echo my feelings. I rarely find that women who carry are fearful about their safety, unless, of course, they are being stalked. I urge women who keep a gun at home to also think about legally carrying one, especially when they're out alone, either walking, riding public transportations or in a car. Regrettably, I've met a number of people, who would not have been raped if they were carrying a gun. But fortunately, I know women who saved themselves because they defended themselves with a gun.

Carrying a concealed weapon is a big responsibility. I do not recommend it for everyone. First, you need to decide how you will conceal your gun so that others don't know you're carrying it and get "freaked out" if they happen to see your Glock or Smith & Wesson peaking out of your jacket pocket. Gun stores sell a number of different purses, fanny packs and even briefcases. Another alternative is to holster your gun and one of the best holsters is a "pancake" holster, which is looped through your belt and "sits" in the small of your back. Try out the various alternatives in the store for functionality as well as fashion design, and you may want to purchase a variety of concealing modes depending on when and where you will be carrying a concealed weapon.

One of the most common questions asked in my classes

is whether the gun should be loaded or unloaded when carrying. A defense gun must be ready to be fired at any moment and therefore it must be loaded when carrying it. If you use a semiautomatic, there should be a round in the chamber.

As Lyn Bates, contributing editor of *Women & Guns* magazine explains, "You can't count on having enough time, in an emergency, to safely draw, then safely rack the slide to chamber a round, then aim and fire if necessary. Modern revolvers are safe to carry fully loaded; if yours is so that that its only safe condition is hammer down on an empty chamber, it is time to get a new carry gun."

In all situations, gun safety is paramount:

1) Keep the gun pointed in a safe direction. Be particularly vigilant when taking out your gun and putting it in its concealed mode;

2) Be aware of all situations. There may be a time that if you're attacked or feel that your life is in jeopardy that you may not be able to shoot in self-defense because you could injure or kill innocent bystanders;

3) In a self defense situation, always keep your finger off the trigger while you bring the gun up and aim it, unless you need to shoot immediately. In some situations, you may need to draw your weapon as a deterrent, but won't need to shoot it;

4) If you're in a gun fight and if you have the opportunity, take cover. Most tactical gun experts contend that if a crime victim takes cover as soon as possible in the face of gunfire, she will survive at an exponential rate. Cover can conceal you and potentially stop a bullet from hitting you. A bush, for example, is not cover, but it can be concealment.

5) Use judgment; Lyn Bates, says that people always ask, "will I be making the right decision?" Bates explains, "Just the fact that you formulate that question, and worry about it, shows that you are a responsible person who is concerned about doing the right thing."

If you're planning on carrying a concealed weapon, you need advanced instruction oriented toward defensive training. I teach an advanced class where you learn how to draw from concealment safely and quickly. It also includes exercises in taking cover so that you are as little exposed as possible in an outdoor gunfight situation. After taking advanced instruction, do continue to practice on an outdoor range going through various scenarios that you've been taught so that you can keep your muscle memory. You can also do the same at home without loading your gun. Always make sure prior to practicing at home that your gun is unloaded. Remember that one of the most important safety rules is never assume a gun is unloaded. Always think it's loaded. Again, before handling a gun, check to see that it is unloaded.

Every state, as well as local jurisdictions within each state, has specific gun laws. Know your state's gun laws. Although there are 38 states that have "shall issue laws," each area has different regulations for carrying a concealed weapon. "Shall issue" statutes require licensing authorities to issue CCW licenses to citizens if they meet specific requirements: background checks, fingerprinting;

Armed & Famous in New York

As of 2003, among the more than 3,600 privileged New Yorkers allowed to legally carry a loaded weapon are actors Robert De Niro and Harvey Keitel, shock-jocks Howard Stern and Don Imus, developer Donald Trump, record executive Tommy Mottola and Channel 5 TV anchor John Roland. Also on the list are ex-Seagrams CEO Edgar M. Bronfman, defense lawyer Barry Slotnick, state Senate Majority Leader Joseph Bruno, Daily News co-publisher Fred Drasner, Manhattan Judge Leslie Crocker Snyder, Arkansas Lt. Gov. Winthrop P. Rockefeller and Assistant state Attorney General Steven Pagones. Ex-top cop Howard Safir and Simon & Schuster publishing czar and author Michael Korda have gun licenses, but they can't legally carry them since they don't have "carry" permits. Their "premise" permit allows them to keep a gun in their homes and demands that when they travel with their weapons, the guns must be unloaded and locked in a safety box, with the ammunition kept separate. Source: Levine Breaking News clean mental health and criminal records, and in a number of states, mandatory training requirements, which may include passing a proficiency test.

By law, there are places where you can't carry a gun. In Texas, for example, a concealed handgun can't be carried into a school, college, hospital, nursing home, church, court, racetrack, sporting event, polling place, or amusement park. Also, some businesses, local government buildings and public transit authorities may display signs barring the carrying of guns. Employers may also stop their employees from carrying a gun while working and some businesses actually have locked individual storage lockers to secure a gun.

There are some states which have "discretionary" licensing, which means a state can deny an individual on arbitrary grounds usually requiring proof of need. New York state, which has "discretionary licensing," varies from jurisdiction to jurisdiction in its licensing requirements, processing time and "need" requirement. New York City is the worst city in terms of law-abiding citizens getting a CCW permit, let alone having a gun in the house!

Fortunately, some states are changing their laws. Recently, Colorado was a discretionary licensing state until its legislature passed "Shall Issue" in March, 2003.

If you don't want to carry your gun in a purse, fanny pack or holster, but want your gun to be handy, it's legal to keep it in the car in some states. Common places to conceal a weapon are in the glove box, but it's not that accessible, in the console between the front seats or under the driver's seat. Another favorite place is on the passenger seat under a jacket or newspaper, but if you stop suddenly the gun can slide off the seat onto the floor making it difficult to retrieve it, if needed. Once you leave the car and you're not taking your gun with you, make sure it's in a secure place and your car windows are shut and the doors are locked!

A few states have reciprocity with other states. If you're lucky and live in South Dakota, for example, the state has agreements with Alaska, Florida (including non-resident permits), Georgia, Indiana, Kentucky, Michigan, Montana, North Dakota, Utah, Missouri, Ohio, (limited to 60 consecutive days) and Wyoming.

Many times a woman, who legally carries a gun can help a loved one and thwart an attack. In September, 2002, in Dallas, Texas, the following story almost seems like it was a scene from a movie. Dr. David Avery and his wife, Patricia, were returning home one afternoon. As Avery backed his GMC truck into his driveway, a green Honda pulled in front of him. A man wearing a mask and brandishing an AK-47 jumped from the vehicle and ordered the 70-year old man to get on the ground. Avery didn't know what would happen to him or his wife as he lay face down on his driveway.

Patricia, who always carries a .38 revolver, without being seen by the assailant, quickly got out of the car and positioned herself behind the passenger side door and squeezed off five shots. Fleeing toward the green car, the masked man returned fire, striking the couple's truck several times, and drove away. The next day, the police recovered the car with what appeared to be a bullet hole in the rear window.

Neither Avery nor Patricia was injured, but police said she might have wounded the gunman. Avery said, "If it wasn't for her being so cool-headed, we would've been in trouble. I told her she was a hero."

Traditionally, men have legally carried a concealed gun and it is only recently that more women are carrying in their purses, pockets or fanny packs. In some respects, the "concealed carry movement" is a women's issue. In fact, according to author and research director of the Independence Institute, Gary Koppel, "about a quarter of those who apply for and receive carry permits are women." When Alaska governor Walter Hickel signed concealed carry legislation in 1993, he said that the constituents he found most compelling were "the women who called and said they worked late and had to cross dark parking lots, and why couldn't they carry a concealed gun?"

Some years ago, I taught two weekend seminars in Anchorage, Alaska, and I was astounded and delighted that the majority of the students had concealed-carry permits and were extremely comfortable toting their guns. I almost had the feeling that everyone carried! One of the women told me during the class that there's an Alaska saying, "If you're a liberal, you carry a .38 and if you're a conservative you carry a .357 magnum!"

Leading women advocates for concealed-carry laws include Texas Sate Representative Suzanna Gratia Hupp, whose parents were murdered a number of years ago in a mass killing in a restaurant in Killeen, Texas; Rebecca John Wyatt, the founder of Safety for Women and Responsible Motherhood; and Marion Hammer, the former president of the National Rifle Association and activist in the Florida concealed-carry debate. Hammer once brandished her handgun to stop a gang of assailants.

A comprehensive study by University of Chicago law professor John Lott, with graduate student David Mustard (*More Guns, Less Crime*, University of Chicago Press) examined crime data for 3,054 counties, and found that while concealed carry reform had little effect in rural counties, in urban counties, it resulted in a substantial reduction in homicide and other violent crimes such as robbery. Additionally, there was a statistically significant rise in no confrontational property crimes, such as larceny and car theft. According to the authors they hypothesized that many criminals decided that the risks of encountering a victim who could fight back had become too high!

Lott and Mustard estimated that if all states that did not have concealed carry laws in 1992 adopted such laws, **there would be approximately 1,800 fewer murders and 3,000 fewer rapes annually. Also, they said that the**

biggest beneficiaries of concealed-carry reform were women, even if they didn't carry guns. Many authorities in the gun movement think that the adoption or improvement of concealed carry laws in more than a dozen states since 1992 may be one of several causes for the decline in murder rates in the nineties.

In fact, in October, 2003, the Associated Press reported, "A sweeping federal review (Centers for Disease Control Report) of the nation's gun-control laws - including mandatory waiting periods and bans on certain weapons - found no proof such measures reduce firearm violence." The analysts also noted after their review of 51 gun laws that "firearms-related injuries" in this country have declined since 1993 despite the fact that "approximately 4.5 million new firearms are sold each year."

Numerous cases now exist about females who legally carry concealed guns and stop a crime because they were carrying at the time of the incident.

One of the best stories was reported in the Post Gazette newspaper and was written by staff writer, Lori Shontz. It occurred in Pittsburgh one early morning on October 15, 2002, when a 42 year-old woman found herself in a rather bizarre situation. Charmaine Dunbar, an off-duty security guard at the University of Pittsburgh, was walking her dog when a man approached her from behind, pointed a gun at her telling her to stand there while he shot her.

"He looked like a monster," she said. He didn't seem human."

Charmaine picked up her dog with one hand and held her other hand up in warning; she was carrying a gun, but did not reach for her it. The man said, "Stand there while I shoot you."

Charmaine's fight mechanism tore through her mind as she hysterically pleaded for her life and then started running. Somehow she hoped that she could dodge the bullets. To her surprise, her loud shouts apparently upset her assailant and he fled in the opposite direction. She yelled out for help and someone called the police. An officer arrived, escorted her home and took a report.

After he left, as Charmaine sat on her sofa reviewing in her head what had just happened to her she began to feel good about her actions. She had survived what she thought was a close call; perhaps she had learned her wily-ness and aggression when she had taken a handgun course so that she could carry a weapon with her for her job. "I just figured, 'Why not start out again?,'" Charmaine said. "Never in my wildest dreams did I imagine that I would see that man again."

While walking, she noticed two men talking on the opposite corner. As she walked up a hill and passed them, soon after one of the men came up behind her. When he caught up with her, Charmaine looked at him and realized he was the man who had threatened to shoot her before.

As nonchalantly as possible, she calmly remarked to the man, "This hill gets to you," and the man agreed. At the top, he was so out of breath, he sat down. Charmaine felt she had a chance to get away and walked more quickly, but then she heard someone running behind her. She turned and saw the man pull a .22-caliber rifle out of his pants and point it at her.

She knew that she needed to fire before he was able to take aim, she steadied her gun and fired twice at his abdomen. He continued to lean over, apparently unaffected, and Charmaine thought, "Oh my God, my bullets didn't work."

Then he stood up, yelled, and fell over. Charmaine ran to her parents' house and returned to the scene with her father. They waited until the police came because she didn't want him to flee.

Charmaine shot a man named Daniel Wesley, 28, who had sexually attacked or tried to attack six women in the previous six weeks. In each of the attacks, the woman was approached from behind, just as Charmaine was. In three of the five incidents, the man mentioned a weapon or the victim actually saw it. Two of the assaults ended in rape, a third in forcing the woman to perform oral sex. According to police, the attacks had steadily grown more violent since they began on September 25. Several nights that week, undercover officers staked out the 8-10 block area in which Wesley had been active, hoping to catch him.

Some detectives even pulled voluntary overtime shifts to catch the attacker.

Police said Wesley might have gotten wise to the undercover police and shifted to a different part of the city, which led to Charmaine's encounter.

The women ranging in age from 10-33 identified Wesley from photos as their attacker.

According to Police Chief Robert McNeilly, Jr., "there was no indication Charmaine was searching for her attacker and she wouldn't be charged."

Charmaine, who is married, the mother of three and the grandmother of one, said she rarely practices shooting. In the past year, she fired her gun twice, once when visiting relatives in Alabama, and a second time on Sept. 14 when she took a recertification course, as required by law.

She spent three years on active duty in the Army beginning in 1980, and learned to fire an M-16. She didn't get a permit to carry her own gun until 1997, when she took a job as a security guard. Through that agency, she worked on a government job where she was required to provide her own gun.

Ever since Charmaine has owned the handgun, she has kept it in her bedroom in case someone breaks in. She also carries it in her car when she goes out at night and in a holster on her right hip – and under her baggy clothes - when she exercises.

Although Charmaine's story never appeared on TV's *Sixty Minutes* or Fox News, she is a maverick. Charmaine stopped a predator of women.

Unfortunately, very few women, or for that matter men, carry guns. For example, in Florida in 2002, 300,603 people held valid concealed gun license holders. Most of them were in the 36-50 age range and 85 percent of the licensees were men, according to State Division of Licensing statistics. In the U.S. only 1 to 4 percent of the adult population legally carry a gun for protection.

I strongly believe that if more and more women had permits to carry a gun there would be far less crimes against women in the next following years.

My position is based on John Lott's data that clearly demonstrates that in those jurisdictions where citizens can legally carry a concealed weapon, rape significantly declines. Also, there's a remarkable story (see *Armed & Female*, pages 15-17) that occurred in Orlando, Florida in 1967, when more than 6,000 women were trained to shoot a handgun by the police department over a six month period. As a result of that training, while most other crimes escalated or remained steady, rape in Orlando fell from a 1966 level of 36 to only 4 in 1967 and stayed at that low level for a number of years, while rape increased throughout the state and the nation. Experts who analyzed the situation contend that the rape rate decreased because of the media publicity and because the women were armed and trained.

VEHICLE IDENTIFICATION ON YOUR VEHICLE

The vehicle identification number of your vehicle, which can be seen through your windshield, has now become the center of attention for crooks. If the number is copied down, and taken to either a car dealer or lock smith, a duplicate key can be made, and your car can be stolen. It is suggested that while your car is parked, to leave a piece of paper or business card over the VIN plate so it cannot be seen.

CHAPTER EIGHT

SAFETY IN YOUR HOME

In one of my gun defense seminars for women in Los Angeles, one of the students, Melanie Blankstone, a single woman, who lives alone in Beverly Hills, asked me what to do after she purchased a handgun and brought it home. Most importantly, I advised her to put the firearm in a safe place—either a portable gun safe or other kind of safe in her bedroom (since she had a large home, I suggested that she have more than one gun in her home)—and then to take the time to strategize on what she would do if an intruder entered her house. Melanie was terrified at the thought of planning for an attack, but I explained that preplanning is necessary because you will behave in an emergency only what you have been trained to do and if you haven't done anything, you may find yourself in fear and total confusion.

SETTING YOUR PRIORITIES

No material possession, whether it's an expensive computer, a flat-screen television, jewelry, or stereo equipment, etc. is valuable enough to protect with lethal force. However difficult it may be to you, let the intruder carry-off your belongings. You only want to use your gun to protect yourself or your loved ones. You own a gun to STOP a violent criminal attack. Don't assume you can intimidate an attacker by brandishing your weapon. If he sees you waiver or have reservations, he may attempt to take it away from you.

One of the most important rules of home defense is DO NOT "clear" your house, which means that if you think someone has entered your home do not go from room to room looking for the bad guy or guys.

According to John P. McFarland (*Combat Handguns* magazine, March, 2004), "Every ex-military person knows that the tactical advantage is with the defender, not the attacker. The defender is difficult to detect because he/she is stationary and hiding behind some type of cover or concealment. The attacker is exposed and therefore subject to ambush. If you attempt to clear your house you have become the attacker and the intruder is the defender."

DETECTING AND RECTIFYING YOUR HOME'S VULNERABILITY TO INTRUDERS

First, do a walk-through in your house. Look for weak areas such as inadequately secured doors and windows. On exterior doors, check for deeply set dead-bolt locks with strike plates, plus sturdy, jimmy-proof locks on all windows, as well as secondary locks or wooden or metal dowels to block sliding glass doors and windows. Also, inspect bathroom windows, as well as garages and basements. When replacing items, don't skimp and buy inexpensive products. Remember, your dealing with your life and the lives of your family. Consider buying a home alarm system with motion detectors, but know that the alarm is a warning device and not a protection system as some security companies claim.

Self defense expert Gila Hayes, explains in the November-December, 1999 issue of *Women & Guns* magazine, "Identify hiding places that could conceal an intruder, waiting to attack when you are off guard or asleep. Remember, a motivated criminal can squeeze into small recesses you might overlook. Try to eliminate hiding areas. For example, coat closets near a front door can be blocked by stacking storage boxes in the bottom, making it difficult to stand inside."

DEVELOPING A SAFE ROOM

A few years ago when the movie *Panic Room* opened there was talk among the Hollywood *cognoscenti* regarding the installation of these rooms in their homes. Actually, the rooms are called "Safe Rooms," but to sell tickets to the movie the screenwriter made up the more exciting term "panic room."

Since 9/11, more people are concerned about home safety. According to the *Wall Street Journal* (March 14, 2003), 300,000 Americans have Safe Rooms. Elaborate Safe Rooms with ventilation systems run by generators, batteries or solar power start at $400,000 and are usually built for wealthy people who have art and jewelry worth millions of dollars or who have to deal with the threat of kidnapping and extortion. A mid-range customized Safe Room developed by Maryland builder, Zytech, costs $26,000.

But you don't have to be wealthy to have your own Safe Room to protect yourself against an intruder. Even though you may have an alarm system, one of your best home defense strategies is to make your bedroom into a Safe Room since most rapes occur at night while you're sleeping.

To do so, you need to install a solid-core door and equip it with a Medeco dead-bolt lock. Then purchase two flashlights along with extra bulbs and batteries and put them inside the room in a place where you can easily access them. Install a second phone line that is not part of the regular house phone system or keep your cell phone well charged in your bedroom. Secure your gun or guns and spare ammunition, as well as soft body armor. Finally, buy a first aid kit and a fire extinguisher.

Check if your bedroom has an escape route to the outside. Then ask yourself the following questions:
1.   Can I get to a neighbor's house and ask for help?
2.   Are my neighbors usually home?
3.   If I need to run down an alley, is it safe?

If you live on the second floor, purchase a rope or chain ladder (I recommend Quick Escape Ladder) so you can leave through the window, and practice climbing down the ladder so you know how to do it in case of an emergency.

Now, let's go over what you need to do if an intruder enters your house, other than through your bedroom.

First, retreat to your Safe Room if not already there, dead-bolt the door, make sure your gun is loaded and call the police from your cell phone or separate phone line. Tell the operator that you have a gun and you're prepared to shoot, if necessary. Follow the dispatcher's instructions and stay on the phone until the police come. When the police arrive, **PUT YOUR GUN DOWN!** The police won't know if you're the bad gun or the good guy. To them, you're a person with a gun and they're as fearful as you are and could shoot you! Again, under no circumstances should you leave the Safe Room and look for the intruder in the house. Remember, exiting the Safe Room could put you at a disadvantage. The dangers are tremendous. Best advice: Wait for the police to arrive. You can give a verbal warning to the intruder: "Get out! We are armed (always say "we" even if you're alone)! We've called the police. You won't be hurt if you leave now!"

If you have children, everything changes. Instead of making your room into a Safe Room, it's better to make your youngest child's room into a Safe Room, because it saves time to bring everyone together in one child's room. When your children are mature enough and can understand the concept of home self- defense, you may want them to create their own Safe Rooms and establish their own escape routes. For now, however, the most important thing is to rehearse responses to various scenarios that may occur. Also, teach your baby-sitters your Safe-Room defense strategy.

If you have a large home, you may want to create a second Safe Room near your kitchen. Or if you use your den or home office frequently, make that a Safe Room, too. Remember, any room can be made into a Safe Room—even a closet. I know women who have made their bathrooms into Safe Rooms because they feel vulnerable while bathing.

If you live in a rental and can't afford to purchase a solid-core door and dead-bolt lock, you can improvise by buying a Door Jammer, which easily screws on to the bottom of your door. Once installed, all you have to do is push the Door Jammer's lever down with your foot and the door can't be forced open. An intruder would have to break through it.

Also, consider installing a Safe Room in your office. I recommend that when you're staying after hours, contact the security guard so that it will be known that you're on the premises.

Unfortunately, in our dangerous times, more precautions need to be taken at home, in the office, in the car, and when you're traveling. The saying, "better safe than sorry" holds true.

YOUR HOME FLOOR PLAN

Certainly, you know the layout of your house better than anybody. You can walk through every room in the dark without tripping over

---

Full Metal Auto

Cars are becoming "Mobile Safe Rooms" for some people, especially celebrities and the wealthy. According to *Newsweek* (March 17, 2003), armored cars are becoming popular in the US since September 11th. Ford introduced the $140,000 Lincoln Town Car BPS—for Ballistic Protection Series—which can stop an AK-47 and block a grenade. GM manufactures an armored Cadillac Deville capable of deflecting bullets from a .44 Magnum. Owners of Cadillac Escalades and Hummer H2s are putting full-metal jackets on their cars at prices ranging from $30,000 to $350,000 above sticker price! If you're interested in outfitting your present car, contact Secure Car W o r l d w i d e : www.securecarworldwide.com or 866-CAR-1481

---

furniture or knocking over lamps, unless you're a very messy housekeeper. You also know the contents of your house better than any stranger, and you are probably capable of feeling your way through the living room to where you know candles are stored should you have a power failure. But, as I mentioned before, you may be surprised to see how many places a stranger could hide, and how quickly someone could enter your house and move through it behind the cover of furniture or appliance.

It will take only a few minutes to sketch the floor plan of your residence with furniture and fixtures in places, and only another few minutes to study the layout for places of cover where you would be able to conceal <u>yourself</u> and take aim on an intruder who was entering your place or moving through a room.

Once you have studied the floor plan for each room, note how the furniture aligns and offers concealed angles from which to shoot toward doors, windows, and hallways. Go to those rooms and crouch alongside or behind the barriers to experience first-hand the cover they offer and the angles afforded.

Select a spot in each room that provides the best vantage point for seeing all entries to the room at the farthest distance from each room. This may be difficult to determine, and you may have to move some furniture to construct such a spot. You may think this is outrageous, but without a secure, concealed point of defense you will lose the tactical advantage in your own home. And without tactical advantage, you may be forced to defend against a surprise attack from an unknown direction, so that the attacker may well overwhelm you and cause you to react with panic and recklessness. Luck becomes your weapon at that point.

FINDING COVER AND SHOOTING ANGLES

Find your vantage point in each room of your house. It must provide you with a cover and a shooting angle to every door and window in the room. It must also be a position from which, if you had to shoot, you would not risk the lives of innocent family members or neighbors behind where your target would be moving. As you study and adjust the layout of your rooms, you have the advantage of preplanning the direction in which you might have to shoot. Find a spot for the living-room couch or reading chair such that, when you hide behind it, you will have a view of entrances to the room and angles to shoot from that will not permit a stray bullet to penetrate a wall into a bedroom or family room or possibly go through a window headed directly for your neighbor's kitchen door. If you cannot find a spot from which every shooting angle would be safe, you must <u>absolutely</u> load your handgun with ammunition which will not penetrate walls.

THINK COVER

According to Paul Markel (*Combat Handguns* magazine, November, 2003), "I was always taught to always 'think cover'. Be 'cover conscious' was the phrase....The question is, what should you do en route to this cover or what if cover is not immediately accessible? Many firearms instructors require their pupils to 'break the plane' after firing only one or two shots. To break the plane the shooters must either move laterally left or right, or they must drop down to a crouch or to a knee. Breaking the plane changes the target picture the bad guy is engaging. Hopefully, this will give you that split second advantage to neutralize the threat. Moving laterally not only takes you out of harm's way for a moment it also allows you to move toward cover."

Practicing lateral movement is not easy since you should do it on an outdoor range with the assistance of an instructor or a friend, who is a shooter. I did lateral movement training at a number of gun training courses, including John Farnam's and Ray Chapman's courses and the Gun Sight school. It's actually fun to do and you come to realize how agile you can be in an emergency situation. Once you've mastered the drill, you can do it at home with an **unloaded gun that you have checked at least twice.** Markel recommends using a solid backdrop, such as a full bookcase for practice.

TACTICAL ADVANTAGE IN YOUR BEDROOM

Locating a position of tactical advantage in your bedroom (and most likely, your Safe Room) is a little more difficult and a lot more critical. More critical because bedrooms are usually arranged in one section of a house, so the shooting angles from within your bedroom can easily lead to penetration of your children's bedrooms. And more difficult because in a bedroom there is usually a minimum of furniture from which to find concealment.

In most bedrooms the bed will be used for a shooting barricade, and must therefore be positioned in the room to give the tactical advantage from a crouch that will provide concealment from shooting angles to all the doors and windows in the room. And that position of the bed must be such that a shot toward the bedroom doors or windows will not have as a background the walls or doors of other, occupied bedrooms. It may take some research and rearranging, but if you have children or family members in the house you must be absolutely sure that your tactical positions within your residence will not compromise the safety of anyone.

REHEARSE YOUR TACTICS

After you have scrutinized your floor plans and gone into each room to establish your vantage points, take a few more minutes to rehearse getting into position in each room at night, with no light coming except through the windows. You will only have to do this rehearsal once, so make it good. In fact, you may want to run through your home tactics one night with your **unloaded gun** in hand, so you can really see the angles and learn the positions.

Again, you will do in an emergency only what you have been trained to do. Think of this practice as training; take it seriously. The object is to learn tactics, eliminate confusion and reverse the surprise advantage your opponent has. Do it once under simulated conditions and you will not forget it should the time come to defend yourself in your home.

TEAMING UP WITH YOUR SIGNIFICANT OTHER OR HOUSEMATE(S) FOR HOME SELF DEFENSE

I have been describing self defense tactics with the idea that you are alone and defending yourself. What about if you're partnered or have a roommate? A mistaken identity shooting can occur, so preplanning and coordination is important. What is their role in an overall home defense strategy? Obviously, two people are better than one; two individuals working together as a team is a far more effective opponent.

According to officer Bob Campbell, "Efficiency is not doubled, it goes up exponentially. A second set of eyes and hands is a great aid in a critical incident." In *Women & Guns* magazine, (September-October, 2002), Campbell explains, "There is more than a tactical advantage in having a reliable, effective partner. The mental component is important. Your gear is subject to failure, but not you partner. A partner is like the duality of backup guns. The synergistic effect of a teammate's presence can defuse a critical incident before it 'breaks bad.' "

If you and your partner team-up, my best advice is to find a qualified instructor, who excels in reality-based training that includes tactics, support and coordination. Total familiarity of your gun is crucial. Furthermore, if each of you own different gun models, you both should be proficient with each other's firearms. Since most self defense situations occur in close proximity averaging about seven feet, the teamwork needs to be practiced within those parameters. As Campbell remarks, "two people training is not standing on the line shooting together."

It certainly is an enormous commitment for both of you to engage in team self defense, but if you're serious about each other's safety, you'll be introduced to a field that previously was only available to SWAT teams and other law enforcement groups. And, it can be downright fun!

Although home defense planning does take time and, it is a procedure that you will not regret if an intruder enters your home.

CHAPTER NINE

SPORT SHOOTING AND HUNTING

SPORT SHOOTING

I don't want to ignore other aspects of gun shooting, which include various sports shooting activities. These group activities can provide you with a new social group and if you're single, there's a good chance you could meet a new "significant other."

Competitive Pistol Shooting

Whether they're shooters or not, most women don't know about the sport of competitive pistol shooting, which was started by the U.S. Congress when it established the National Board for the Promotion of Rifle Practice (NBPRP) in 1903. The organization added pistol matches the following year. In 1936, the NRA conducted its first National Championships and is the governing body for precision pistol shooting in the U.S.

Hundreds of matches are held throughout the country and one of the best ways to get started is to attend a match to see if this sport is right for you. (The "Coming Events" section of *Shooting Sports USA* magazine lists all upcoming NRA-sanctioned tournaments). Also, if there is a shooting club in your area make arrangements to go to one of its practice sessions.

A standard course of fire for pistol competition is a "3-gun aggregate." This is fired with .22 caliber rimfire, an unspecified caliber centerfire, and .45 caliber handgun. But, a competitor doesn't need to own three different guns. In most tournaments, people enter and fire only one of more stages of the aggregate. Many competitors entering the complete aggregate bring only .22 and .45 caliber handguns since the .45 caliber may be used for the center-fire stage.

You don't need a lot of expensive equipment to get started in competitive pistol shooting. A .22 caliber-rimfire handgun

(either an autoloader of a revolver) and eye and ear protection is all you need. A 20X to 30X spotting scope is
helpful to you so you can see your shots on the target to
make sight corrections.

Match grade ammo is available at gun stores, but costs
more than standard loads. Many serious competitors
handload their own ammunition (excluding .22 rimfire),
since the loads can be "customized" for a particular gun.

Another type of competitive handgun shooting is Defensive Pistol Shooting (10,000 members worldwide), which
simulates "real world" self defense scenarios that typically
require shots from 3 - 20 yards and often requires the
shooter to change firing points and shoot from awkward
positions. Defensive Pistol matches offer diversity and truly
test both accuracy and speed. During my initial training, I
competed in a few of these events and really enjoyed the
challenge of playing "cops and robbers."

Shooters competing in Defensive Pistol events or Tactical
matches are required to use practical autoloaders or revolvers, such as a Beretta, Glock, Sig Sauer or Smith & Wesson,
(.9mm/.38 Special or larger caliber) and holsters or fanny
packs that are suitable for self-defense use. Practical concealed carry type holsters are necessary. No "competition
only" equipment is allowed since the goal is test the skill
and ability of an individual, not her equipment or games-
manship. Defensive Pistol competition is divided into four
divisions so all popular pistols and revolvers have a place
to compete competitively.

Even people with disabilities have the opportunity to
compete. In 1997, the NRA started the National Rifle Asso-
ciation-Beeman Grand Prix Championship, a 12 city championship tour that has been especially attractive to female
and minority participants of all ages.

Every event is conducted at a different location (hotel
ballrooms, high school gymnasiums, sporting goods stores,
rehabilitation hospitals and at a sportsmen's show with over
23,000 spectators) with widely varying range conditions.

Actually, the biggest problem shooters face is traveling to and from the events, especially if they're in wheelchairs. Winning an event title is an incredible feat on many levels. For information, contact the National Rifle Association.

Competitive Shooting For Kids

You may have thought that gun competitions for kids didn't exist, but on the contrary, there are numerous junior competitions throughout the U.S., culminating in the National High Junior Pistol Matches (there are also rifle competitions). And perhaps even more surprising is that in 2001, 2002 and 2003 a female high school student, Teresa Meyer, came in first place beating out the boys! Based on her accomplishments, Teresa was invited to the Olympic Training Center in Denver by the assistant coach for further training and a possible position on the USA Team. What does she offer for other young shooters, especially female juniors? "Try it! Stick with it. It's fun." (*Women & Guns*, January-February, 2004)

Shooting is excellent training for young people: It's very personal, it challenges the individual and tests personal motivation. Also, shooting hones the senses, sharpens the eye, and focuses concentration, which is often lacking in kids. For more information on competitive shooting for young people, contact your state NRA or the national office in Fairfax, Virginia.

If you're unsure about your children using live fire, consider airgun competition. Since 1965, the Daisy Corporation and the U.S. Jaycees have cosponsored a program that begins with shooting events in local hometowns and ends with an international event. More than 2,000 Jaycee chapters (250,000 kids) throughout the country conduct supervised classes to teach girls and boys ages 10-14 proper gun handling and marksmanship. Kids can go on to compete in state and regional competitions and then those winners compete at the International BB Gun Championship Match, the oldest and largest continuous airgun competition in the world.

Hunting

Although hunting is not a self-defense issue, more and more women are taking up hunting . According to the National Sporting Goods Association (2001), of the 19.2 million active hunters in the United States, 13% or 2.4 million are female. (Hunters were defined by the NSGA through a nationwide survey of persons 7 years old and older who had participated more than once in the past year).

I was given the opportunity to hunt wild boar in Central California, but I never took up the challenge. Was I afraid? Well, frankly I was. People had whispered in my ear that wild boars were extremely aggressive and I better know how to shoot fast and well. That stopped me.

Do I plan to hunt in the future? Yes, I definitely want to try it. But, first I need to practice shooting a rifle and a shot gun. Since I've spent years shooting a handgun and teaching handgun proficiency, I've never made the time to practice long gun shooting. I've shot skeet and trap at various NRA events years ago, but unfortunately, I never mastered either sport.

In general, a majority of women abhor the idea of hunting and get into the "Bambi Syndrome" when they think of hunting deer. Many women don't know that all across the nation, whitetail deer numbers have skyrocketed. Five hundred years ago, the deer population was kept in check by predators — wolves, cougars, bobcats, bears, coyotes, and Indians. But since large scale development and the restraints on hunting, coupled with the decline of natural predators, the national whitetail herd now exceeds 30 million!

According to James Swan, author of *In Defense of Hunting*, "Mushrooming herds are becoming a wildlife-management nightmare. Lyme disease, carried by deer-borne ticks, has been reported in 43 states. Deer can also carry tuberculosis, as well as chronic-wasting disease, the mysterious brain-eating illness that belongs to the same family of illnesses as mad-cow disease and Creutzfield-Jacob disease.

"Insurance companies report over 500,000 deer-car collisions annually, resulting in about a hundred human deaths. (Let us not forget that more people are hurt and killed by deer than by any other species of North American wild game.) Several studies place the total number of deer hit by cars at four to six times the number reported. The average insurance claim for a deer-car collision is $2,000. Deer damage to agriculture crops and landscaping costs more than $1 billion a year."

Swan says that hunting is the most economical and effective way to limit the size of herds and control the problems that their explosive growth has caused. Many anti-hunters don't know that most hunters believe it is wrong to kill game that will not be eaten. To waste a game animal like a deer is a sin to them. At the same time, we need to shoot more deer, but what to do with all the venison?

There's a terrific solution that is being implemented, which shouldn't anger anyone who is anti-hunting. Several organizations have been channeling surplus venison and other game meat to the needy. The USDA estimates that in 2,000, 33 million people (22% of all children were living in poverty) didn't have enough food to meet their basic daily needs. One nation-wide Christian faith-based group, Farmers and Hunters Feeding the Hungry, has coordinated and paid for the processing and distribution of over 1,400 tons (12 million servings) of venison for the last seven years. Hunters for the Hungry is another group of venison-donation charters across the U.S. It has collected and donated over 1.5 million pounds of venison since 1991. Safari Club International's Sportsmen Against Hunger focuses on both national and international big-game hunting and estimates that its wild-game meat and other donations help feed some 230 million people a year.

If you've considered taking up hunting, all 50 states

require people to take a hunter-education course to get a hunting license. As Swan says, "(You'll) nourish you soul, (and) be able to continue a very old tradition of sharing wild game with those who need it."

BIBLIOGRAPHY & RESOURCES

Atwood, Margaret, *The Handmaid's Tale*, Random House, 1986

Ayoob, Masad, *In The Gravest Extreme*, Police Bookshelf, 2001

Bates, Lyn, "Murder and the Reasonable Woman," Women & Guns, March-April, 2004: 12-57

Baty, Kathleen, *A Girl's Gotta Do What A Girl's Gotta Do*, Rodale, 2003

Chapman Academy of Practical Shooting, 4350 Academy Rd., Hallsville, MO., 65255, 800-847-0588

Citizens Committee for the Right To Keep and Bear Arms, Liberty Park, 12500 N.E. Tenth Place, Bellevue, WA., 98005, 800-486-6963

Combat Handguns, Harris Publications, 1115 Broadway, NY, NY, 10010

Executive Security International, Gun Barrel Square, 2128 Railroad Ave., Dept. Web, Rifle, CO., 81650, 888-718-3105

Gottlieb, Alan, *The Gun Rights Fact Book*, Merril Press, 1989

Gun Owners of America, 8001 Forbes Place, #102, Springfield, VA, 22151, 703-321-8585

Gun Sight Academy, 2900 W. Gunsite Rd., Paulden, AZ, 86334, 928-636-4565

Gun World, 265 S. Aviation Drive, Orange, CA., 92868

Hayes, Gila, *Effective Defense*, 2nd Printing, The Firearms Academy of Seattle, 2004

Jews for the Preservation of Firearms Ownership, P.O. Box 270143, Hartford, WI, 53027, 262-673-9745

Hoff, Linda, "All in the Name of Hunting," Woman's Outlook, October 2003: 30-66

Impact & Prepare, 800-345-5425

Kasper, Shirl, *Annie Oakley*, Oklahoma Press, 1992

Kates, Don, Polsby, Dan, "Of Genocide and Disarmament,"
Journal of Criminal Law and Criminology 86, (Fall
1995): 247-256

Kelly, Caitlin, *Blown Away: American Women and Guns*, Pocket
Books, 2004

Kleck, Gary, Kates, Don B., *Armed: New Perspectives on Gun
Control*, Prometheus Books, 2001

Kopel, David B. *The Samurai, the Mountie, and the Cowboy*,
Prometheus Books, 1992

Korwin, Alan, *Gun Laws of America*, Bloomfield Hills Press,
2003 Lethal Force Institute, P.O. Box 122, Concord, NH.,
03302, 800-624-9049

Lott, John R., Jr., *The Bias Against Guns: Why Almost Everything
You've Heard About Gun Control Is Wrong*, Regnery,
2003

Lott, John R., Jr., *More Guns Less Crimes: Understanding Crime
and Gun Control Laws*, University of Chicago Press, 2000

MacNutt, Karen, L. "Bare Arms," Women & Guns, March-April,
2004: 50-52

National Rifle Association, 11250 Waples Mill Road, Fairfax,
VA., 22030, www.nra.org

Markel, Paul, "Under Fire-Your Move," Combat Handguns,
November 2003: 16-95

McFarland, John, P., "Home Defense Alert," Combat Handguns,
March 2004: 58-59

Quigley, Paxton, *Armed & Female*, St. Martin's Press, 1990

Quigley, Paxton, *Not An Easy Target: Paxton Quigley's Self-
Protection for Women*, Simon & Schuster, 1995

Rauche, Walt, *Practically Speaking: An Illustrated Guide: The
Game, Guns and Gear of the International Defensive
Pistol Association with Real-World Applications*, Raunch
and Company, 2004

Riley, Glenda, *The Life and Legacy of Annie Oakley*, Oklahoma

Press, 1994

Second Amendment Foundation, 267 Linwood Avenue, P.O. Box 488, Buffalo, NY, 14309

Second Amendment Sisters, 900 R.R. 620 S, Suite C-101, Box 228, Lakeway, TX, 78734

Silk & Steel Foundation, 1770 Bucks Hills Road, Southbury, CT, 06488

Single Action Shooting Society, 877-411-SASS, www.sassnet.com

Stange, Mary Zeiss, ed., *Heart Shots: Women Write About Hunting*, Stackpole Books, 2003

Stange, Mary Zeiss, Oyster Carol K., *Gun Women: Firearms and Feminism In Contemporary America*, New York University Press, 2000

Students for the Second Amendment, 12911 Vidorra Circle, Dept. WG, San Antonio, TX, 78245, www.sf2a.org

Wilson, R.L., *Silk And Steel: Women at Arms*, Random House, 2003

Woman's Outlook, National Rifle Association, P.O. Box 420648, Palm Coast, FL, 32142

Women & Guns, P.O. Box 488, Buffalo, NY., 14209, 716-885-6408

Zelman, Aaron, Stevens Richard W., *Death By "Gun Control:" The Human Cost of Victim Disarmament*, Mazel Freedom Press, Inc., 2001

Would you like more copies of
Stayin' Alive
Armed & Female in an Unsafe world

Just mail in our simple-to-use form here to order more copies!

-OR-

Call (425) 454-7009

DISCOUNT SCHEDULE

1 copy	$15.00	25 copies	$250.00
5 copies	$67.00	50 copies	$425.00
10 copies	$120.00	100 copies	$800.00

Merril Press
P.O. Box 1682
Bellevue, WA 98009

Please send me_____copies of Stayin' Alive.
Enclosed is my check or money order in the amount of
$_____.

-OR-

Please charge my: ☐Visa ☐Mastercard ☐AMEX ☐Discover

Number: _____**Expires:** _____

Signature:_____

Print Name:_____

Street:_____

City: _____ **State:** _____

Zip:_____ **Phone:** (_____)_____

GEORGE W. BUSH
SPEAKS TO THE NATION

Since the beginning of his presidency, George W. Bush has been blowing his critics away with the power and finesse of his speeches. Attacking momentous issues confronting American and the world, he has delivered historical and inspiring orations that are captured in this new book. Alan Gottlieb has selected President Bush's most pivotal speeches to be enjoyed for a lifetime.

POLITICALLY CORRECT GUNS...

is a take-no-prisoners invasion of the Gun Control crowd's territory, lobbying humor grenades at their hypocrisy, bombing their misplaces zeal with cleaver vignettes, and surrounding their antigun rhetoric with such pointed parody that even Gun-Banner Bill Clinton will have to laugh at himself.

Alan Gottlieb has done it again-defending our gun rights with wits and facts, this time with some really strange but true stories.

This hilarious parody of gun control is filled with political cartoons and gags, but hitting home a serious point about the individual right to keep and bear arms. It exposes the hypocrisy of the elite who want armed guards for themselves but no weapons for you. **Just mail in our simple-to-use form here to order copies, or call: (425) 454-7009.**

- -

DISCOUNT SCHEDULE

1 COPY	$14.95	25 COPIES	$250.00
5 COPIES	$67.00	50 COPIES	$425.00
10 COPIES	$120.00	100 COPIES	$800.00

Please send me_____copies of *Politically Correct Guns*. Enclosed is my check or money order in the amount of $_____.

Please charge my: ☐Visa ☐Mastercard ☐AMEX ☐Discover

Number: _____Expires: _____

Signature:_____

Print Name: _____

Street: _____

City: _____ State: _____ Zip:_____

Phone: (_____)_____

Mail to: Merril Press, PO Box 1682, Bellevue, WA., 98009

Politically Correct Hunting

An irreverent romp through the world of hunting, poking a little fun at hunters and a lot of fun at their animal rights opponents. Posing as an alphabetical dictionary of

hunting lore, Politically Correct Hunting dispenses jokes, tall tales and homey wisdom.

As Jim Zumbo, Editor of Outdoor Life, says: "Politically Correct Hunting is a fun book that should be on every hunter's night-stand. Ken Jacobson's wit will keep you amused, informed and entertained. This book is loaded with tips, jokes and some downright good philosophy."

Just mail in our simple-to-use form here to order copies, or call: (425) 454-7009. Mail to: Merril Press, PO Box 1682, Bellevue, WA 98009:

DISCOUNT SCHEDULE

1 COPY	$14.95	25 COPIES	$250.00
5 COPIES	$67.00	50 COPIES	$425.00
10 COPIES	$120.00	100 COPIES	$800.00

Please send me_____copies of *Politically Correct Hunting*. Enclosed is my check or money order in the amount of $_____.

Please charge my: ☐Visa ☐Mastercard ☐AMEX ☐Discover

Number: _____Expires: _____

Signature:_____

Print Name: _____

Street: _____

City: _____ State: _____ Zip:_____

Phone: (_____)_____
